The New Evangelization

The New Evangelization

Overcoming the Obstacles

EDITED BY

Steven Boguslawski, OP

AND

Ralph Martin

Paulist Press
New York/Mahwah, NJ

Translations of the Scripture quotations contained herein vary according to each author.

Cover and book design by Lynn Else

Library of Congress Cataloging-in-Publication Data

    The new evangelization : overcoming the obstacles / edited by Steven Boguslawski and Ralph Martin.
      p. cm.
    ISBN 978-0-8091-4532-4 (alk. paper)
    1. Catholic Church—Missions. 2. Missions. 3. Catholic Church—Doctrines. 4. Evangelistic work—Catholic Church. I. Boguslawski, Steven C. II. Martin, Ralph, 1942–
    BV2180.N489 2008
    266'.2—dc22

                                          2008011101

Published by Paulist Press
997 Macarthur Boulevard
Mahwah, New Jersey 07430

www.paulistpress.com

Printed and bound in the
United States of America

Contents

Contents

Introduction

One of the most important legacies of John Paul II's pontificate is his urgent and repeated call to a "new evangelization."

Pope John Paul II first called for a new evangelization in 1983 in Haiti—a new evangelization that would be "new in ardor, methods, and expression." This call became a major theme of his pontificate. In 1992 he addressed all the bishops of Latin America on the occasion of the 500th anniversary of Columbus's discovery of the New World and its subsequent evangelization. Again, the pope called for a new evangelization, explaining it more fully.

> The new evangelization does not consist of a "new gospel."…Neither does it involve removing from the Gospel whatever seems difficult for the modern mentality to accept. Culture is not the measure of the Gospel, but it is Jesus Christ who is the measure of every culture and every human action. The new evangelization has as its point of departure the certitude that in Christ there are "inscrutable riches" (Eph 3:8) which no culture nor era can exhaust, and which we must always bring to people in order to enrich them….These riches are, first of all, Christ himself, his person, because he himself is our salvation.[1]

In 1990, Pope John Paul II chose the occasion of the twenty-fifth anniversary of the conclusion of the Second Vatican Council to issue the most important recent magisterial document on evangelization, the encyclical *Redemptoris Missio* (Mission of the Redeemer). In this important encyclical, the pope made clear that this new evangelization has its roots in the documents of the Second Vatican Council. Pope John XXIII, Pope Paul VI, and Pope John Paul II all understood this council to have been called to foster renewal in the Church so that the Church can be more effective in showing Christ to the world, that is, for the sake of renewal and evangelization. In this document John Paul II made a very strong statement: "I sense that the moment has come to commit all of the

Church's energies to a new evangelization and to the mission *ad gentes*. No believer in Christ, no institution of the Church, can avoid this supreme duty: to proclaim Christ to all peoples" (*Redemptoris Missio* 3).

When the pope spoke of the new evangelization, he primarily meant the need to reevangelize those traditionally Christian countries that have been weakened by a process of secularization. In these countries or regions, there may be many people who bear the name of Catholic but who do not follow Jesus as disciples and friends. John Paul II saw an urgent need to call to conversion the many millions of nominal Catholics throughout the world. In a document he issued at the end of Jubilee Year 2000 that presented his vision for the third millennium, *Novo Millennio Ineunte*, he made the striking statement: "Even in countries evangelized many centuries ago, the reality of a 'Christian society' which, amid all the frailties which have always marked human life, measured itself explicitly on Gospel values, is now gone" (*Novo Millennio Ineunte* 40).

Pope John Paul II also called for a renewed evangelization directed to those who have never had a chance to hear the gospel—*ad gentes*—the unevangelized peoples of the world. He asked the whole Church at every level to review its plans and priorities to make sure that evangelization is at the center.

In light of this urgent and repeated call, Cardinal Adam Maida, archbishop of Detroit, announced in 2003 that he would like Sacred Heart Major Seminary to be a place where "heralds" for the new evangelization would be formed. This is now a guiding principle as the seminary revises existing programs and implements new ones, both for the approximately 100 seminarians and for the 450 lay students.

One of the new degree programs has been authorized by the Congregation for Catholic Education and Seminaries in conjunction with the University of St. Thomas (the Angelicum) in Rome to grant a Licentiate in Sacred Theology (STL) with a focus on the new evangelization. The seminary now has students from six different countries enrolled in this STL program.

In order to mark the establishment of this pontifical degree program, Cardinal Maida asked the seminary to plan and implement a convocation that would bring together the best existing scholarship on the new evangelization and make it available to a broad audience of leaders in the Church, both clergy and lay.

Introduction

This convocation was convened in the archdiocese of Detroit in March of 2005. More than four hundred attendees from all over the United States and Canada responded enthusiastically to the top-quality presentations from some of the best experts in the field. The particular theme of the convocation was "The New Evangelization: Overcoming the Obstacles." The purpose was to examine some of the major doctrinal, spiritual, and pastoral challenges that need to be faced for the new evangelization to be effective. There was a widespread demand for the publication of these excellent presentations and this volume is the outcome.

We are happy to present these truly excellent presentations as a response of Sacred Heart Major Seminary to the urgent call to a new evangelization.

—*Fr. Steven Boguslawski, OP*
—*Ralph Martin*

NOTE

1. Pope John Paul II, "Address to Bishops of Latin America," *L'Osservatore Romano*, English Language Edition, October 21, 1992, p. 7, section 6.

Vatican II and Evangelization

Avery Cardinal Dulles, SJ

Responding to the Protestant Reformers, the Council of Trent at some points sounded a surprisingly evangelical note. In its discussion of the authorities to be used for teaching and conduct, that Council declared that the gospel was the source of all saving truth and moral discipline, and was to be preached to every creature.[1] By this emphasis on the gospel and evangelization, the Catholic Church could have claimed to be, in its own way, evangelical.

In the next few centuries, however, Catholics shied away from speaking about the gospel and evangelization, since Protestant churches had appropriated these terms. The Catholic Church was content to be known as the Church of tradition, law, priesthood, and sacraments rather than the Church of the Word of God.

Vatican II made a decisive shift toward evangelical Catholicity, but this shift was scarcely noticed by early commentators, most of whom interpreted the work of the Council in traditional Catholic categories. Vatican II became known for what it had said about the distribution of power in the Church, the reform of the liturgy, ecumenism, interfaith relations, and dialogue with the modern world—all themes of little or no interest to Evangelicals.

In *Evangelii Nuntiandi,* issued in 1975, ten years after the close of Vatican II, Pope Paul VI gave a radically different interpretation, emphasizing proclamation and the gospel. The objectives of the Council, he wrote, "are definitively summed up in this single one: to make the Church of the twentieth century ever better fitted for proclaiming the gospel to the people of the twentieth century." In this apostolic exhortation, Pope Paul VI fulfilled a request of the 1974 Assembly of the Synod of Bishops, which asked him to gather up the fruits of its labors, giving "a fresh forward impulse" and inaugurating what he called "a new period of evangelization" (*Evangelii Nuntiandi* 2). Rereading the Council documents in light of this statement, we can find considerable support for the pope's contention.

The two great dogmatic constitutions of Vatican II, those on the Church and on revelation, open on a strongly evangelical note. *Lumen Gentium*, the Dogmatic Constitution on the Church, begins with the assertion that Christ is the light of all the nations, and that the Church as his sacrament strives to shed his radiance on all human beings, which brightens her countenance as she proclaims the gospel to every creature (*Lumen Gentium* 1). *Dei Verbum*, the Dogmatic Constitution on Divine Revelation, begins with a strikingly kerygmatic passage. The Church, it affirms, "hearing the word of God with reverence and proclaiming it confidently," wishes to hand on Christ's message "so that by hearing the message of salvation the whole world may believe; by believing, it may hope; and by hoping, it may love" (*Dei Verbum* 1).

The missionary spirit expressed in these passages permeates nearly all the documents of Vatican II. It is most evident, of course, in the splendid but rather neglected decree on the Church's missionary activity, *Ad Gentes Divinitus*. But the same spirit is evident in the Decree on the Apostolate of the Laity (*Apostolicam Actuositatem*), which expounds at some length the ways in which lay men and women can suffuse the temporal sphere with the light and energy of the gospel, bearing witness to Christ by their words and their conduct. Passages in the Council documents that deal with bishops, priests, and liturgy emphasize the proclamatory dimension of the sacred ministry and the sacraments, especially that of the Eucharist, which is described as "the source and apex of the whole work of preaching the gospel" (*Presbyterorum Ordinis* 5). The Pastoral Constitution on the Church in the Modern World, *Gaudium et Spes*, while speaking extensively of dialogue, gives equal attention to proclamation as a means of making the light of the gospel shine everywhere, fostering freedom and charity, and transforming the human race into the family of God (*Gaudium et Spes* 32, 41, 92).

In order to make these observations more concrete, we may pose a series of questions about evangelization: its nature, its purposes, its bearers, its addressees, and its methods. All of these questions can, I believe, be adequately answered from documents of Vatican II.

What Is Evangelization?

The word *evangelization* originally meant the proclamation of the good news that the day of redemption had arrived. The gospel (*evangelion, evangelium*) is the good news, the saving message, heralded by an "evangelist." On many occasions the Council cited the words of Paul to the Romans: "The gospel is the power of salvation to those who believe" (*Unitatis Redintegratio* 21; see *Lumen Gentium* 19, 26; *Dei Verbum* 17; *Dignitatis Humanae* 11). In the course of the centuries, the term *gospel* was increasingly objectified, so that it came to stand for the entire content of revelation. Vatican II sometimes used the term to signify the basic message to be proclaimed, but sometimes more broadly, meaning the fullness of revelation given in Jesus Christ. Unlike Lutherans, Catholics do not divide revelation into law and gospel. God's revealed law is part of the gospel.

Evangelization accordingly has two senses. In the narrow sense it means the announcement of the global Christian message to those who do not believe, that is to say, primary evangelization. But in a broad sense it means everything that brings human life and the world under the sway of God's Word. In this second sense evangelization practically coincides with the total mission of the Church. Normally, if not in every case, Vatican II used the term *evangelization* in the narrow sense, to mean the action of announcing Christ rather than of bringing his influence to bear upon diverse persons and situations through education, pastoral care, and social action.

Paul VI in *Evangelii Nuntiandi* opted for the broader meaning. He taught that evangelization includes preaching and teaching, reconciling sinners to God, and perpetuating Christ's sacrifice in the Mass (*Evangelii Nuntiandi* 14). John Paul II went back to a somewhat narrower meaning. He spoke of the first evangelization that occurs in missionary activity, and of reevangelization and new evangelization in parts of the world where Christianity has ceased to be a vital influence, but he did not include pastoral care under the rubric of evangelization (*Redemptoris Missio* 2, 33–34).

Why Evangelize?

Christians, who confess Christ to be the Savior of the world, should have no difficulty in finding motives for evangelization in any of the forms just mentioned. Vatican II frequently quoted the final charge of the risen Christ to the apostles: to preach the gospel to all the nations of the world. This missionary mandate, as expressed in Mark 16:15, is quoted or referenced at least a dozen times in council documents (*Lumen Gentium* 1, 16, 19, 24; *Dei Verbum* 7; *Unitatis Redintegratio* 2; *Orientalium Ecclesiarum* 3; *Ad Gentes Divinitus* 1, 5, 38; *Presbyterorum Ordinis* 4; and *Dignitatis Humanae* 13). Matthew 28:19–20, which reiterates the same mandate, is cited only slightly less frequently (e.g., *Lumen Gentium* 17, 19, 24; *Dei Verbum* 7; *Ad Gentes Divinitus* 5; and *Dignitatis Humanae* 13, 14). Obedience to the Lord's command is, therefore, the primary motive for evangelization.

Supplementing the argument from authority, the Council proposed intrinsic reasons for missionary activity: it contributes to the glory of God and the salvation of human beings. God is glorified when his saving work in Christ is acknowledged, when hymns of praise and thanksgiving rise to him, and when people shape their lives according to his teaching. In turning to Christ, men and women benefit themselves. Christ delivers them from the power of sin. As they receive the gifts of grace, they are made sharers in God's inner trinitarian life (*Lumen Gentium* 17; *Ad Gentes Divinitus* 7–8).

The decree *Ad Gentes Divinitus* teaches that missionary activity is an intrinsic demand of the Church's own catholicity. Tending by her very nature to express her catholicity, she realizes herself by proclaiming God's Word to the nations and thereby contributing to the establishment of God's kingdom everywhere (*Ad Gentes Divinitus* 1).

Vatican II was careful not to reject authentic values that existed in the world *before* it was touched by the gospel. Evangelization, it declared, preserves everything good that is to be found in human cultures or religions, frees it from admixture with evil, and elevates it to a higher plane. "Whatever good is in the minds and hearts of men, whatever good lies latent in the religious practices and cultures of diverse peoples, is not only saved from destruction but is also healed, ennobled, and perfected unto the glory of God, the confusion of the devil, and the happiness of man" (*Lumen Gentium* 17; see *Gaudium et Spes* 58).

The Council did not fail to address the question of the necessity of the Church. She is indeed necessary because God has associated her inseparably with Christ as his Mystical Body. Having made her a universal sign of salvation, he uses her as his instrument for the redemption of all *(Lumen Gentium* 9). All who attain salvation, therefore, depend on the mediation of the Church as well as upon Christ, the divine mediator. Those who are in a position to recognize Christ as savior are bound to believe and to confess him by joining the Church *(Lumen Gentium* 14).

To the question whether it is possible for people to be saved without actually hearing and accepting the good news of Jesus Christ, the Council answers with a qualified affirmative. If, with the help of God's grace, they do what they can to conform to God's will, God will make it possible for them to attain salvation in some way known to himself *(Lumen Gentium* 16, *Ad Gentes Divinitus* 7, *Gaudium et Spes* 22.) But if they hear and accept the gospel, they will have many additional helps to salvation: the guidance of revelation, the pastoral care of the Church, and the graces of the sacraments. Lacking these helps, people are often deceived into exchanging the truth of God for a lie *(Lumen Gentium* 16).

The comprehensive vision of the Council is splendidly displayed in *Lumen Gentium* 17, which states as follows:

> The Church is compelled by the Holy Spirit to do her part towards the full realization of the will of God, who has established Christ as the source of salvation for the whole world. By the proclamation of the gospel, she prepares her hearers to receive and profess the faith, disposes them for baptism, snatches them from the slavery of error, and incorporates them into Christ so that through charity they may grow into full maturity in Christ....
>
> In this way the Church simultaneously prays and labors in order that the entire world may become the People of God, the Body of the Lord, and the Temple of the Holy Spirit, and that in Christ, the Head of all, there may be rendered to the Creator and Father of the Universe all honor and glory.

5

Who Should Be Evangelized?

Vatican II stated many times that all men and women are to be evangelized. It made no exceptions, because the rationale for evangelization applies to all, no matter what their race, nationality, gender, or social condition.

Since the Council, some theologians have suggested that Christians ought not to trouble adherents of other religions by proclaiming Christ to them. Since it is possible for such persons to be saved without becoming Christians, it is argued, we should leave them in good faith, helping them to live good lives in their own religious tradition. As a general policy, this practice would be unsound and contrary to the teaching of Vatican II. As a matter of pastoral prudence, however, it is sometimes advisable to wait for an opportune moment before confronting certain persons or groups with the claims of the gospel. They may need to be better prepared in order to hear it fruitfully.

Some contemporary Christians have maintained that there is no need to evangelize Jews, because Jews already enjoy a salvific covenant relationship with God. Having treated that question elsewhere,[2] I do not want to go through that whole discussion again, but for present purposes it may suffice to say that the teaching of Vatican II makes no exception for Jews, simply saying that the gospel is to be proclaimed to every creature. Jesus Christ died for all and wills that all come to a knowledge of the truth. Believing Jews, of course, are not in the same condition as pagans. They already have the Word of God as given in the Law and the prophets. But by acknowledging Jesus as the promised Messiah and Lord to whom their ancestors looked forward, Jews give additional glory to God and enter into the blessings of the new and perfect Covenant prefigured by the old (*Lumen Gentium* 9).

The question could be raised whether Catholics should evangelize other Christians. According to the teaching of Vatican II, these others are not fully initiated into the Body of Christ. Baptism is only the first sacrament of initiation and demands to be completed by the Eucharist (*Unitatis Redintegratio* 22). Full communion requires acceptance of the Church's entire system and admission to the Eucharist, the sacrament of full communion (*Lumen Gentium* 14). Since the whole creed and the dogmas of the Church, as well as the sacraments and pastoral government, pertain to the gospel, it follows logically that Christians who are not Catholics still require additional evangelization. But Vatican II, as I have mentioned, did not seem to use the term *evangelization* in this broader sense.

Missionary activity includes evangelization and the planting of the Church, but it does not include the pastoral care of the faithful or undertakings aimed at the restoration of unity among Christians (*Ad Gentes Divinitus* 6; see *Unitatis Redintegratio* 4). Having said that, the Council pointed out that both these activities are closely connected with missionary activity and consequently with evangelization. Pastoral care arouses zeal for evangelization in individuals and communities. Division among Christians is a serious impediment to evangelization, since it blocks the way to faith for many. "Hence, by the same mandate which makes missions necessary, all the baptized are called to be gathered into one flock, and thus to be able to bear unanimous witness before the nations to Christ their Lord" (*Ad Gentes Divinitus* 6; see *Unitatis Redintegratio* 1).

By the same token it may be asked whether Catholics themselves are still in need of evangelization. Many who have been baptized into the Catholic Church have not yet heard the gospel convincingly proclaimed. Some who have been catechized have never captured the basic Christian vision. They know a good many doctrines of the Church but seem never to have encountered the living Christ. They could certainly profit from hearing the kind of proclamation that is designed to bring nonbelievers to faith.

In passages dealing with evangelization, Vatican II did not speak to the question of unevangelized Catholics, except perhaps in one passage. In the Decree on the Mission Activity of the Church, the Council alluded in passing to the problem of "dechristianization." It said that changes can occur in previously evangelized areas that call for a renewal of missionary activity (*Ad Gentes Divinitus* 6).

Even without using the term *evangelization* for ministry to marginal and inactive Catholics, the Council called attention to their need for a fresh encounter with the gospel. In Scripture reading, preaching, and Bible study, the faithful continually renew and energize their commitment. "The force and power of the word of God is so great that it remains the support and energy of the Church, the strength of faith for her sons, the food of the soul, and the pure and perennial source of spiritual life" (*Dei Verbum* 21).

Pope Paul VI, in *Evangelii Nuntiandi,* On Evangelization in the Modern World, would take the next step. The Church herself, he declared, stands in constant need of being evangelized, converted, and renewed in order that she may evangelize the world with credibility (*Evangelii Nuntiandi* 15). The Church's evangelizing activity, he said, cannot ignore Christians who have drifted away from religious practice (*Evangelii Nuntiandi* 56).

Pope John Paul II, in his encyclical *Redemptoris Missio,* would expatiate on this theme. He devoted a section of that encyclical to the reevangelization of peoples with ancient Christian roots, whose adherence to the Church is merely nominal and who live lives far removed from Christ and the gospel. They are not objects of missionary activity in the strict sense, said the Pope, but are in need of reevangelization (*Redemptoris Missio* 33).

Who Should Evangelize?

In recent centuries Catholics have commonly looked upon evangelization as the task of persons who receive a special call to become preachers or missionaries. The main body of the faithful considered that their task was not to extend the faith but to receive God's grace and live according to the gospel. Vatican II made a new step forward. At many points it insisted that the whole Church is missionary and that every member is obliged to take part in disseminating the gospel. "The obligation of spreading the faith," it stated, "is imposed on every disciple of Christ, according to his ability" (*Lumen Gentium* 17; see *Apostolicam Actuositatem* 35). But the obligation, it recognized, does not rest upon all in the same way. People in different states of life have different obligations.

The Dogmatic Constitution on the Church opens its discussion of the episcopal office with the words: "Among the principal duties of bishops, the preaching of the gospel occupies an eminent place. For bishops are preachers of the faith who lead new disciples to Christ" (*Lumen Gentium* 25). The diocesan bishop, it states, must be "ready to preach the gospel to all (see Rom 1:14–15) and to urge his faithful to apostolic and missionary activity" (*Lumen Gentium* 27). The Decree on the Mission Activity of the Church teaches that "the responsibility to proclaim the gospel throughout the world falls primarily on the body of bishops....[Missionary activity] is a supremely great and sacred task of the Church" (*Ad Gentes Divinitus* 29). Both individually in their dioceses and in councils and conferences, bishops are required to stimulate, organize, and direct evangelization.

Diocesan priests carry on the work of ministry in parishes, extending and applying the ministry of the bishop. In their pastoral activity they are exhorted to "stir up and preserve among the faithful a zeal for the evangelization of the world" (*Ad Gentes Divinitus* 39). Both the Decree on the Renewal of Religious Life and the Decree on the Mission Activity of the Church mention the prominent role traditionally played by religious orders, both active and contemplative, in missionary evangelization (*Perfectae Caritatis* 20; *Ad Gentes Divinitus* 18; see *Lumen Gentium* 44).

Other documents, such as the Decree on the Apostolate of the Laity, strongly emphasize the involvement of the laity in the evangelization of the settings in which they live and work: "The laity are called in a special way to make the Church present and operative in those places and circumstances where only through them can she become the salt of the earth" (*Lumen Gentium* 33). "This evangelization," it adds, "that is, this announcing of Christ by a living testimony as well as by the spoken word, takes on a specific quality and a special force in that it is carried out in the ordinary surroundings of the world" (*Lumen Gentium* 35). The Christian family can be an outstanding example of testimony to Christ and the gospel (ibid.).

The Council also encouraged the laity to cooperate in ministries designed to build up the Church herself. Some lay persons, it noted, receive a special vocation to work with the hierarchy in teaching Christian doctrine, in liturgical services, and in the care of souls (*Apostolicam Actuositatem* 24). Organizations such as Catholic Action exemplify the collaboration of lay persons in the apostolate proper to the hierarchy (*Apostolicam Actuositatem* 20).

Ways of Evangelization

Among the many paths of evangelization, the most obvious is the preaching of the gospel, which the Decree on the Mission Activity of the Church describes as the "chief means" of implanting the Church.

But when circumstances prevent the direct and immediate announcement of the gospel, Christians can bear witness to Christ very effectively by charity and works of mercy (*Ad Gentes Divinitus* 6). The laity, in particular, can exercise a fruitful apostolate by their conduct in the areas of their labor, profession, studies, neighborhood, and social life. And according to the Decree on the Apostolate of the Laity, they will look for opportunities to announce Christ to their neighbors through the spoken word as well (*Apostolicam Actuositatem* 13).

Proclamation of the gospel should always take account of particular cultural contexts. Without using the term *inculturation*, *Gaudium et Spes* conveyed the idea. "This accommodated preaching of the gospel," it declares, "ought to remain the law of all evangelization" (*Gaudium et Spes* 44). The gospel has a transformative impact on the cultures it encounters. "By the very fulfillment of her mission, the Church stimulates and advances human and civic culture....[The gospel] strengthens, perfects, and renews them [cultures] in Christ" (*Gaudium et Spes* 58; see 61). Popes Paul VI and John Paul II would have a great deal more to say about the evangelization of cultures.

Evangelization can also take the form of social action, even though the proper and proximate goal of such activity is inner-worldly and natural. By promoting right order of values in their earthly activities, Christians practice faithfulness to the gospel and win respect for it. Allowing their whole lives to be permeated by the spirit of the beatitudes, they promote justice and charity in society (*Gaudium et Spes* 72).

Vatican II did not find it necessary to caution against the danger of confining evangelization to social action. But after the emergence of liberation theology in the late 1960s, Paul VI felt obliged to speak out against the temptation to reduce the mission of the Church to the dimensions of a simply temporal project (*Evangelii Nuntiandi* 32). John Paul II likewise warned against "kingdom-centered" theories of mission, which imperiled the true notion of evangelization by advocating the advancement of peace, justice, freedom, and brotherhood without any reference to Christ and the Church. The Kingdom of God, said the Pope, "cannot be detached either from Christ or from the Church" (*Redemptoris Missio* 18). In so teaching, John Paul II was in full accord with the theology of Vatican II, which closely identified the Kingdom of God with the Church, even while keeping the two concepts distinct (*Lumen Gentium* 3, 5, etc.).

Another problem that has arisen since the Council is a false opposition between evangelization and dialogue. A tension can arise since dialogue is not directly ordered to conversion, but there is no opposition because, as we read in the Decree on Ecumenism, both proceed from the wondrous providence of God (*Unitatis Redintegratio* 4). Pope John Paul II was sufficiently concerned to say that interreligious and ecumenical dialogue should not be seen as substitutes for evangelization. "The Church," he wrote, "sees no conflict between proclaiming Christ and engaging in interreligious dialogue" (*Redemptoris Missio* 55).

Vatican II at a number of points disavowed what it called unworthy methods of evangelization. No one should seek to gain converts by appealing to merely temporal motives, by offering false promises, by physical or psychological coercion, or by falsely demeaning other churches or religions. According to the Declaration on Religious Freedom, the adherence of faith must always be physically and psychologically free (*Dignitatis Humanae* 2, 4, 10; *Ad Gentes Divinitus* 13).

The New Evangelization

Pope John Paul II in 1983 announced his program for what he called "the new evangelization."[3] He took the program for this initiative in substance from Vatican II, under the guidance of Paul VI's interpretation. But he was able to strengthen and dramatize the project in his many apostolic journeys.

The U.S. Bishops have taken some steps to implement the program of the new evangelization,[4] but they have not as yet found a way of overcoming the resistance of the culture against any such initiatives. The reigning culture in countries like our own, tending to promote subjectivism and relativism in religion, discourages efforts to win new adherents to any specific faith. It is hard for Catholics to keep from absorbing the general approbation of religious pluralism.

St. Paul quoted the psalmist as saying, "I believed, and so I spoke" (2 Cor 4:13; see Ps 116:10). Belief, where it is healthy and strong, naturally expresses itself in words and actions. If Catholics do not evangelize, the fundamental obstacle does not lie so much in the surrounding culture as in themselves. Having failed to nourish their faith by study, prayer, and contemplation, many have become weak and flabby in their adherence to the gospel and the Church. If they personally grasped the vision of faith, they would joyfully give witness to Christ, even at the cost of wealth, honors, and life itself. Perhaps their faith is weak because they have not tried to share it. As John Paul II wisely observed, "Faith is strengthened when it is given to others" (*Redemptoris Missio* 2).

The agenda of Vatican II, Paul VI, and John Paul II still remains to be properly understood and implemented. The Council called upon every Christian, whether bishop, priest, religious, or lay, to evangelize by word, by personal example, and by helping to transform society according to the mind of Christ. An increasing group of young Catholics, I believe, is sensing the urgency of this project. In recent visits to colleges and seminaries I have been struck by the numbers of enthusiastic youthful believers who put evangelization at the top of their priorities. May their tribe increase!

NOTES

1. H. Denzinger and A. Schönmetzer, *Enchiridion Symbolorum, definitionum et declarationum de rebus fidei et morum*, 1501 (Freiburg im Breisgau: Herder, 1963), 364–65.

2. Avery Cardinal Dulles, "The Covenant with Israel," *First Things* 157 (November 2005): 16–21.

3. Pope John Paul II, "The Task of the Latin American Bishop," Address to the Bishops' Council of the Latin American Churches, Port-au-Prince, Haiti; *Origins* 12 (March 24, 1983): 659–62.

4. In response to Paul VI's *Evangelii Nuntiandi*, the National Conference of Catholic Bishops established a Committee on Evangelization. In 1992, the Conference also published various documents connected with the Fifth Centenary of the Evangelization of the Americas, and in November 1992 released a national plan for evangelization under the title "Go and Make Disciples." The Conference issued pastoral statements on World Mission in 1986 and 2005.

2

Current Theological Obstacles to Evangelization

Avery Cardinal Dulles, SJ

My assignment is not to speak on evangelization itself but rather on the doctrinal obstacles that make it difficult to evangelize in the United States today. Because I cannot cover all the obstacles in this one lecture, I shall concentrate on one attitude that is pervasive in our culture. It is an exaggerated form of egalitarianism that puts every religion, every conviction, and every moral practice on the same level, giving no higher status or authority to any particular creed or group.

There are indeed certain basic human rights given equally to all men and women. But because society is made up of different types of persons having different roles and functions, some have rights and duties that others do not. God, moreover, can freely bestow gifts on some that he withholds from others. A false egalitarianism ignores these differences, and attributes the same rights and gifts to all. An obvious instance, much debated in our day, is the so-called right to same-sex marriages. But this is only one instance of an evil that is pervasive in specious forms, subtly undermining authentic Christian proclamation. In what follows I shall call attention to a number of cases.

Last year I had an occasion to address a group of Christians and Jews on the subject of the covenant. To my surprise I found out that some of the audience objected to the very idea of a covenant on the ground that it would place those who received it in a position of moral superiority. A properly democratic ethos, they seemed to feel, meant that God should treat every individual as equal. In reply I tried to point out that our God is a personal God, who freely bestows gifts on those he loves and who makes us collaborators in his salvific plans. Friendship with God, besides being a great benefit, is also a call to service, since more will be required of those who have received greater gifts. But my answers seemed to make no impression on my objectors.

I mention this incident because the attitude I found among that audience is not untypical of Americans today. Almost all of us are under the influence of the egalitarian individualist culture in which we live. Christians, including Catholics, are inclined to believe that religion is a human construction, an effort to penetrate to some degree into the mystery of the divine. Christians, Jews, Buddhists, Hindus, Muslims, and the rest are all doing about the same thing. God has not bestowed any special favors on any of them.

This attitude, as I see it, is the most fundamental obstacle to evangelization. Evangelization rests on the supposition that the Christian religion is a uniquely precious gift of God. This is indeed the teaching of Scripture; it is also the faith of the Catholic Church, affirmed by Popes and councils down through the centuries. We do not make up a religion according to our own ideas and wishes. The message we believe and proclaim is the gospel of Jesus Christ faithfully handed down in the Church.

Scripture and Tradition teach unequivocally that God has been pleased to form a covenant people upon whom he showers rich blessings. God teaches them about himself and his plan of salvation and nourishes them spiritually with holy practices and sacraments. From very ancient times the Israelites were God's people. Since the death and resurrection of Jesus, the Church of Christ has been the new people of God, the New Israel, the people of the New Covenant. It is not a closed society, but open to all. God loves everyone and wants all to come to the truth. But he wants this to take place through the mediation of those who already believe.

We are, therefore, presented with two antithetical points of view. According to the Christian view, the Church is the people that God has gathered to himself in Jesus Christ. The members of the Church are commissioned to spread the faith, gathering new members from all the nations of the earth. The Church, therefore, is essentially an evangelizing community.

14

Our secular culture promotes the opposite point of view, which maintains that no human community enjoys a privileged relationship with God. Everyone has a right to reject religion altogether, to join any existing religious group, or to found a new sect, as he or she thinks best. There exists no such thing as a deposit of faith, nor is there any agency capable of declaring authoritatively what is contained in the Word of God.

Whether people see the necessity of evangelization depends on which of these two points of view they adopt. For those who adopt the first, it seems perfectly evident that evangelization is a high priority. For those who adopt the second, evangelization is of doubtful value and could even be offensive. Only the first attitude, of course, is authentically Christian and Catholic. But the leveling mentality that is dominant in our secular culture is a powerful undertow that may drag under Christians, including Catholics. Unless they are thoroughly schooled in Christian doctrine, they tend to adopt the attitudes of their fellow Americans.

The prevalent egalitarian humanism has enormous doctrinal implications. Most fundamentally, it undermines the doctrine of revelation and portrays religion as a purely human construct. Christian faith, as understood in the Catholic tradition, is a positive response to revelation, a joyful submission of the mind and heart to God and his word. Those who receive revelation have sure answers to many questions that would otherwise be very difficult or impossible to answer. It would be irrational and ungrateful to reject God's gift because we want to be like everyone else. Our faith, far from harming our fellow human beings, equips us to guide, instruct, and benefit them. We could not evangelize anyone unless we were confident of having something important to give.

The two contrasting attitudes lead to very different views of salvation. According to Christian orthodoxy, God brings about salvation by sending his divine Son as redeemer of the world. Those who accept him as Savior, believing and following his teaching, will attain the eternal life he came to give. Since faith is the gateway to saving truth, Christians have powerful motives to spread the faith, that is, to evangelize.

The democratic egalitarian view sets all religions on the same level, just so many human efforts to speak of the divine. This view leads

15

to an attitude of religious indifferentism. Some say that, while Jesus may be the Savior of Christians, other religions have other savior figures, the Lord Buddha, the Lord Krishna, or some other real or mythical personage. Non-Christians can work out their salvation, whatever that may be, wherever they are. Why should we try to convert them to Christianity if it is just one of many options?

The New Testament leaves no room for debate about which of the two views is the Christian one. It states: "The Father has sent his Son as the Savior of the world" (1 John 4:14); "For God so loved the world that he gave his only Son, so that everyone who believes in him may not perish but may have eternal life" (John 3:16). Paul repeatedly insists that there is but one God, the Father, and one Lord, Jesus Christ (1 Cor 8:5–6). There is only one mediator between God and humans, the man Jesus Christ, who gave himself as a ransom for all, and God wants everyone to come to this truth and be saved (1 Tim 2:4–6). Christians are sent to the whole world, to make disciples of every nation (Matt 28:19–20).

The Second Vatican Council strongly reaffirmed the biblical view. At one point it declared: "The Church believes that Jesus Christ, who died and was raised up for all, can through his Spirit offer man the light and strength to measure up to his supreme destiny. Nor has any other name under heaven been given to man by which it is fitting for him to be saved. [The Church] likewise believes that in her most benign Lord and Master can be found the key, the focal point, and the goal of all human history" (*Gaudium et Spes* 10). In the year 2000, the Congregation for the Doctrine of the Faith reminded Catholics that belief in Jesus Christ as the sole and universal Savior is an indispensable element of the Church's faith (*Dominus Iesus* 13).

Christianity, therefore, does not admit that there are many lords and redeemers, as the egalitarian view would have it. Owing its existence to divine revelation, Christianity is not just one more of the world's religions. While respecting all that is true and healthy in other religions, Christianity holds that they are deficient to the extent that they fail to acknowledge Christ, the Savior of the world, and that they fail to make use of the means of grace that Christ has entrusted to the Church.

Equally harmful are the effects of the leveling mentality on ecumenical relations. The cultural atmosphere of our world inclines us to say that all churches and ecclesial communities, no matter what their tenets may be, are equally legitimate. The Church of Christ, according to this view, has been fragmented into a multitude of denominations, no one of which can claim to have the fullness of Christianity. Even Catholics frequently speak as though it makes no great difference whether a person be Protestant, Catholic, or Orthodox. They sometimes speak as though a multiplicity of mutually complementary churches were the will of Christ himself.

The Catholic Church has never accepted this outlook. It has insisted, and continues to insist, that the Church of Christ subsists in its fullness in the Roman Catholic communion and nowhere else (*Lumen Gentium* 8). The Catholic Church—and she alone—is equipped with the fullness of the means of salvation. All the blessings of the New Covenant have been entrusted to her alone, and whatever elements of the true Church survive in other communions derive from the Catholic fullness and belong by right to the Catholic Church (*Unitatis Redintegratio* 3). These points, clearly stated by the Second Vatican Council, were reaffirmed by the Congregation for the Doctrine of the Faith in its declaration *Dominus Iesus.*

The work of reconciling dissident Christians to the Catholic Church should be seen as continuous with primary evangelization, which consists in the proclamation of the basic Christian message. Catholics should have the courage to declare with Vatican II that their Church has been made necessary by God, and that anyone who is in a position to see this has an obligation to become fully incorporated into her (see *Lumen Gentium* 14; *Dignitatis Humanae* 1). Until people have accepted the fullness of Christian revelation as proclaimed by the Catholic Church, their evangelization is not yet complete.

In our egalitarian culture, confusions have arisen regarding the nature of dialogue. Some believe that, for dialogue to occur, the parties must cease to hold their own doctrines with certitude and be prepared, as a result of the dialogue, to modify or renounce their faith. One author declares: "Dialogue is not possible if any partners enter it with the claim that they possess the final, definitive, irreformable truth."[1] Treating their own commitments as tentative, they look for a doctrinal compromise. Each participating group, according to this theory, should be prepared to surrender some of its own traditions for the sake of concord.

According to Catholic understanding, however, theological dialogue seeks not pragmatic compromise but agreement in the fullness of truth. Dialogue does not exclude proclamation, but includes an element of proclamation, because the parties ask each other to explain their respective positions. There is no reason why convinced believers should be excluded from dialogue or why believers should pretend to be uncertain of their own positions.

Still another point at which contemporary democratic thinking impedes evangelization is its conception of the Church. It looks upon the Church as a community of equals who govern themselves from below. The "people of God" would choose their own rulers, who would then be accountable to the people they govern. Many American Catholics would like the Church to become more democratic. Some changes in this direction might be possible and desirable, but we cannot alter the fact that the government of the Catholic Church is essentially hierarchical, not congregational.

Jesus Christ gave authority to the Twelve Apostles, with and under Peter as their head, and the apostles, as we know, ordained bishops as their successors. According to the Second Vatican Council, "By divine institution, bishops have succeeded to the place of the apostles as shepherds of the Church....He who hears them, hears Christ, while he who rejects them, rejects Christ and him who sent Christ" (*Lumen Gentium* 20, quoting Luke 10:16). The ruling authorities perpetuate themselves by cooption. The Church is democratic only in the sense that people from the lowest ranks are eligible to be appointed to the highest positions. There is no hereditary ruling class: slaves can and have become Popes.

Within the college of bishops, the bishop of Rome, as Pope, enjoys supreme authority. He has jurisdiction over each and every Catholic, including the bishops, and has authority to define doctrine on his own initiative. In turn, Holy Scripture and Tradition greatly restrict the discretion of the Pope himself. He is protected against error in his solemn acts by the power of the Holy Spirit, by the prayer of Jesus, and by the abiding presence of the Lord with the apostolic hierarchy.

The hierarchical style of government is well suited to a society that has the task of preserving and passing on a sacred deposit of faith. The hierarchy has the strength to resist pressures to reconstruct the Church in the image of modern secular society. Our Lord warned that Christians should not be like salt that has lost its savor. They should not fear to be a sign of contradiction.

Another point of tension between the Church and contemporary culture is the sacramental principle. Before ascending to his Father, Christ made provision for his continued presence and activity on earth through ritual signs, or sacraments. In every act of sacramental worship, the principal minister is Christ himself. The sacraments give the Church public social structures. The priest, as the ordinary minister of various sacraments, takes the part of Christ, who acts in and through him. We ought not to look upon the sacraments as lifeless things, but as actions of the living Lord.

In recent years Catholics have been sharply divided on the issue of the reservation of the ordained priesthood to men. This is another instance in which the revelation of God, constantly and universally interpreted by the Church, conflicts with the contemporary egalitarian spirit.

The sacraments, like the gospel itself, are unmerited gifts of God. The Jews of old had the oracles of God, the covenants, and the promises (Rom 9:4). Christians are privileged to hear the gospel so that they may call upon the name of the Lord and be saved (Rom 10:13–17). Baptism brings about a real incorporation into the Body of Christ, and the Eucharist makes us mystically one with him whom we receive. The sacraments of initiation are not reserved for the few, but are available to all who choose to turn to Christ and belong to his Church. One of the most powerful motives for evangelization is to bring more people into the intimate union with the Lord that the sacraments make possible. We should be on guard against letting our appreciation of the sacraments be eroded by the secular egalitarian mentality, which minimizes the gifts of God and extols human initiative.

Finally, it must be recognized that the individualistic secularity of our age is also having an unhealthy impact on eschatology. Cardinal George Pell, Archbishop of Sydney, Australia, at the 2001 Assembly of Bishops, commented on what he called "the considerable silence and some confusion [regarding] Christian hope especially as it touches the Last Things, death and judgment, Heaven and Hell. Limbo seems to have disappeared. Purgatory slipped into Limbo, Hell is left unmentioned, except for terrorists and infamous criminals, while Heaven is the final and universal human right; or perhaps just a consoling myth."[2]

Hans Urs von Balthasar popularized the idea that we may hope that no one ever goes to hell. Rightly or wrongly, he is often interpreted as though he believed that in the end all men and women attain to the joys of heaven. Priests and theologians frequently give the impression that the doctrine of hell is a medieval superstition rather than an essential component of the gospel. In so doing, they may well be doing Satan's work because the fear of hell occupied a central place in the preaching of Jesus.

Instead of further pursuing the question of hell, I would like to concentrate on limbo, which has recently become a subject of intense debate. The International Theological Commission (ITC) has been preparing a statement on the fate of infants who die without baptism. On December 27, 2005, the *New York Times* carried a front-page story with this caption: "Limbo, an Afterlife Tradition, May Be Doomed by the Vatican." The same article was elsewhere reprinted under the headline: "Roman Catholic Church Rejects Longstanding Concept of Limbo." When the ITC document was finally published on April 20, 2007, the press reports were again misleading. The *New York Times* the next morning carried the headline, "Pope Closes Limbo." The article reported, again inaccurately, that the document had been signed by Pope Benedict XVI and that it effectively did away with the doctrine of limbo.

I have personally talked with several members of the International Theological Commission and they inform me that the press reports are, to say the least, premature. The document is still in the process of revision. What's more, the ITC, being simply a study group, has no authority to change Catholic doctrine. It is not an organ of the Magisterium. Its documents are never signed by the Pope. Besides, the statement in question does not flatly reject the idea of limbo. It states that limbo has been and remains a possible theological opinion, but correctly points out it is only one of a number of theories that have been debated over the centuries. The document does, however, register a preference for another hypothesis—that we may hope for the salvation of babies who die without baptism, even though we cannot affirm that they are saved. In this respect the ITC study leans toward the kind of egalitarianism to which I have been referring. Only time will tell whether in this respect the ITC is yielding too much to the spirit of the times.

A considerable body of doctrine concerning the fate of unbaptized infants has been accumulated over the centuries.[3] The Greek Fathers, while asserting the necessity of baptism for salvation, wrote very little about the fate of children who die without baptism. Gregory of Nyssa is the exception because he composed a short treatise on the subject. He speculated that such infants would escape the torments of hell, but he did not teach that they were eligible to receive the beatific vision. In the West, St. Augustine took a more sober view. On the grounds that everyone is conceived in a state of original sin, and that baptism is the remedy for original sin, he concluded that unbaptized infants would be eternally lost, but would be punished less severely than those guilty of personal sin. Many theologians in the early Middle Ages followed Augustine, but in the High Middle Ages theologians such as Peter Abelard, Peter Lombard, Albert the Great, Thomas Aquinas, and Bonaventure took a more optimistic turn. They held that the souls of unbaptized infants, although not capable of receiving the beatific vision, would not suffer any positive affliction. They would pass into a state of relative happiness, which some of them called limbo. These great doctors of the Church were followed by many of the leading theologians of the next few centuries, including Leonard Lessius, Francis Suarez, and Alphonsus de Liguori, some of whom depicted life in limbo in very appealing colors.

Limbo, it should be noted, is not a third place in addition to heaven and hell. Technically, it is part of hell. The Latin term *limbus* means "outer fringe, or margin"—in this case, the border of hell itself. Hell is defined primarily by the deprivation of the beatific vision, the *poena damni*.

Official Catholic teaching has tolerated both the strict Augustinian view and various theories of limbo. In the Middle Ages, several ecumenical councils—those of Lyons II (1274)[4] and Florence (Decree for the Greeks, 1439)[5]—taught that persons who die with only original sin are excluded from the kingdom of heaven, but are not punished in the same way as those who die in personal sin. Pope John XXII taught the same in a letter to the Armenians of 1321. By persons who died with only original sin, the councils and Popes evidently meant unbaptized infants, since all adults would die either in a state of grace or in a state of personal mortal sin.

In its Decree for the Jacobites, the Council of Florence taught regarding children: "Since no help can be brought to them by another remedy than through the sacrament of baptism, through which they are snatched from the dominion of the devil and adopted among the sons of God, [the holy Catholic Church] advises that baptism ought not to be delayed for forty or eighty days…but should be conferred as soon as can be done conveniently."[6] The Council of Trent taught that, since the promulgation of the gospel, it was impossible for anyone to be justified without sacramental baptism or the desire for it.[7] Infants presumably could not have the required desire.

None of these documents specifically mentions limbo, but all of them are open to it. Since the time of Trent, limbo has received increasing favor. Any number of particular councils, catechisms, and textbooks could be cited, but I shall confine myself to three papal statements.

Defending the orthodoxy of those who accepted limbo, Pope Pius VI in 1794 condemned the Jansenist Synod of Pistoia on a variety of counts, including its charge that the doctrine of limbo was "a Pelagian fable."[8]

Pius X in 1905 published a catechism in which he declared: "Infants who die without baptism go to limbo, where they do not enjoy the sight of God, but also do not suffer; this is because, having original sin, and it alone, they do not merit heaven, but neither do they merit purgatory or hell."[9]

Pope Pius XII in 1951 made a weighty statement to a congress of midwives. He taught that while an act of perfect charity could supply for baptism in the case of an adult, that way was not open to children. Hence, he declared, "In the present disposition there is no other means of communicating this [supernatural] life to the child, who has not yet the use of reason."[10]

To sum up the tradition, we may say that two opinions have been permitted. The first was the older Augustinian opinion that the souls of unbaptized infants are punished with the fires of hell, but less severely than those who died in personal mortal sin. The second view, which gradually gained a virtual consensus, is that such souls pass into a state of relative happiness that may be called limbo. Partisans of both theories agreed that children who die without baptism do not receive the beatific vision, unless perhaps God should make an exception in a singular case, such as the sanctification of John the Baptist in the womb.

Limbo is not, and never has been, a settled Catholic doctrine. It is a hypothesis to answer a question that divine revelation does not directly answer. If it is rejected, we have to ask what is being substituted for it and why. A couple of examples may indicate the current mentality.

Father Raniero Cantalamessa, the preacher to the Papal Household, recently declared: "Let us forget the idea of limbo as the place without joy or sadness in which children [who] are not baptized will end up. The fate of children who are not baptized is no different from that of the Holy Innocents, which we celebrated just after Christmas. The reason is that God is love and *wants all to be saved*, and Christ also died for them."[11]

Father John Catoir, former head of the Christophers, is not untypical in writing: "It always bothered me that innocent babies were in some way ineligible to receive the fullness of God's love. Now I know better. Catholics today do not have to believe in Limbo. There is one place of eternal rest and that is Heaven."[12]

One wonders on what basis this new theory is proclaimed. Do we today have some new insight into the gospel that was denied to all previous generations of Catholics, or are we being swept up by the spirit of the times, which so easily casts aside tradition and substitutes human desires as the norm of truth? We should be slow to change what Popes, councils, and saintly theologians have been teaching for many centuries. We may hope that unbaptized infants go to heaven, but we have no assurance that they do.

The *Catechism of the Catholic Church* says about the best that can be said. It lays down the principle: "The Church does not know of any means other than Baptism that assures entry into eternal beatitude" (*Catechism of the Catholic Church* 1257). On the ground that God is not bound by his sacraments, the faithful may hope that God will mercifully admit unbaptized children to the beatific vision. Yet the Church, according to the *Catechism*, takes care not to prevent little children from "coming to Christ through the gift of holy Baptism" (1261). The *Catechism* thus avoids belittling the importance of infant baptism. The casual assumption that infants are saved without either faith or baptism raises serious questions about the whole economy of salvation.

In some quarters it is being held that aborted babies go directly to heaven. This is a particularly dangerous opinion because it can encourage the practice of abortion. Expectant mothers are tempted to think it is better for the baby to be aborted than to be born into a very difficult situation.[13] Already in 1599 Pope Sixtus V issued an apostolic constitution, *Effraenatum*, in which he listed among the evils of abortion the fact that it prevents the aborted child from attaining the beatific vision.[14]

23

My discussion of limbo has been much longer than its relative importance for my topic would seem to require. But it is a current example of the tendency I am deploring. The temptation is to minimize the distinctive gifts of the Church, including the salvific importance of Christian faith and the sacraments. The new evangelization can succeed if Christians joyfully accept the gospel as it has been handed down. New developments in theology are not excluded, but they must grow out of what has been taught and believed by our forebears in the faith. We must always be on guard against proposing our own preferences as though they were the Word of God.

NOTES

1. Paul F. Knitter, *No Other Name? A Critical Survey of Christian Attitudes toward the World Religions* (Maryknoll, NY: Orbis, 1990), 211.

2. *L'Osservatore Romano*, English edition, November 7, 2001.

3. For the history of the doctrine, one may consult A. Gaudel, "Limbes," *Dictionnaire de Théologie Catholique* 9:760–72; A. Michel, *Enfants morts sans Baptême* (Paris: Téqui, 1954); and George J. Dyer, *Limbo: Unsettled Question* (New York: Sheed & Ward, 1964).

4. H. Denzinger and A. Schönmetzer, *Enchiridion Symbolorum, definitionum et declarationum de rebus fidei et morum*, 858 (Freiburg im Breisgau: Herder, 1963).

5. Ibid., 1306.

6. Ibid., 1349.

7. Ibid., 1524.

8. Ibid., 2626.

9. Pope St. Pius X, *Catechism of Christian Doctrine*, ed. Eugene Kevane (Middleburg, VA: Notre Dame Institute Press, 1974), 17. The pope made the use of this catechism obligatory for the Roman Province. By "hell" he evidently understood the state in which those who die with personal mortal sin are punished.

10. Dyer, *Limbo*, 153–54.

11. Father Raniero Cantalamessa commenting on the Gospel for the Feast of the Baptism of Jesus, January 8, 2006. Text obtained from *Catholic Online* (www.catholic.org), January 18, 2006.

12. John Catoir, Column, *St. Louis Review,* February 7, 1997. I am indebted to James Likoudis for this reference.

13. Ralph Martin, "Believing and Praying: The Power of Homilies," *Homiletic & Pastoral Review* 104 (December 2003): 64–66, at 66.

14. Sixtus V, Constitution *Effraenatum*, October 29, 1588, in Pietro Gasparri, ed., *Codicis Iuris Canonici Fontes*, vol. 1 (Rome: Typis Polyglottis Vaticanis, 1923), 308–11, at 308.

3

Who Can Be Saved? What Does Vatican II Teach?

A Response to Cardinal Dulles

Ralph Martin

Cardinal Dulles claims that the cultural atmosphere of "egalitarian humanism" has brought with it an attitude toward religious truth that sees it primarily as a "purely human construct" rather than a matter of divine revelation. He identifies the subsequent "religious indifferentism" as fundamentally undermining the truth claims of Christianity, eroding the foundation for evangelization. While noting the strong biblical, traditional, and magisterial support for the uniqueness of Christ's identity and salvific role and that of the Church, Cardinal Dulles chooses to spend a significant part of his presentation on examining the theological hypothesis of limbo. He does this for several reasons: It is a topic that the International Theological Commission recently studied; several widely publicized news reports and well-known figures in the Church have declared that the outcome is not in doubt, and that unbaptized infants surely go to heaven; and it is an example of a doctrinal issue that has direct bearing on evangelization.

The questions concerning limbo touch on the reality and significance of original sin, on how the redemptive sacrifice of Christ is applied, and on whether faith and baptism are truly required, in some meaningful sense, for participation in the joy of heaven. My own concern would be not so much in defending the theological hypothesis of limbo as in not ignoring the profound theological "facts" that the hypothesis of limbo is attempting to correlate. The question of limbo also touches on our attitude toward divine revelation. There is a temptation—sometimes because of what we believe to be human compassion—to leap to unwarranted conclusions. We must assume that there are important reasons why some things have been revealed to us in our present condition and some things have not been. We must respect the silence of God as well as his speech. It is not compassionate to present as certain what can only be hoped or prayed for. Nor is it respectful of revelation. Nor is it without pastoral implications.[1]

I would like, however, to take up a theme that Cardinal Dulles touches on but chooses not to pursue—that of hell. In the previous chapter, Cardinal Dulles states quite strongly, and quite correctly, I believe, "Rightly or wrongly, he [von Balthasar] is often interpreted as though he believed that in the end all men and women attain to the joys of heaven. Priests and theologians frequently give the impression that the doctrine of hell is a medieval superstition rather than an essential component of the gospel. In so doing, they may well be doing Satan's work because the fear of hell occupied a central place in the preaching of Jesus."[2] In these two sentences Cardinal Dulles has identified a doctrinal confusion that has quite significant implications for evangelization.

There is certainly a very widespread impression among many Catholics today that virtually everybody will end up in heaven, with possibly a few, truly awful exceptions going to hell. One could correctly, I believe, identify this prevailing mentality as a "culture of universalism." Let me elaborate. I travel quite a bit in my work and am exposed to the opinions of many Catholics. If I were to describe the prevailing worldview among most Catholics in North America, Europe, and Oceania today, I would describe it like this: "Broad and wide is the way that leads to salvation and almost everybody is traveling that way. Narrow is the way that leads to hell and hardly anybody is traveling that road." Or to put it another way, "Many are called and virtually everybody is chosen."

The unfortunate thing about this prevailing worldview is that it is exactly the opposite of what Jesus indicates is the truth about our situation: "Enter through the narrow gate; for the gate is wide and the road is easy that leads to destruction, and there are many who take it. For the gate is narrow and the road is hard that leads to life, and there are few who find it" (Matt 7:13–14; see also Luke 13:23–30); and, "For many are called, but few are chosen (Matt 22:14).

In these brief remarks it is not possible to explore all the legitimate exegetical and theological questions that such texts raise, but I believe that Cardinal Newman makes a point that we should keep in mind as we deal with such questions. No matter what the scriptural warnings may end up meaning, the few can never mean the many (and the many can never mean the few). There is a limit to reinterpretation: "Of course we must not press the words of Scripture," Newman said. "We do not know the exact meaning of the word 'chosen'; we do not know what is meant by being saved 'so as by fire'; we do not know what is meant by 'few.' But still the few can never mean the many; and to be called without being chosen cannot but be a misery."[3]

While there are important exegetical and theological questions concerning the question of hell and the possibility of going there, there are also important pastoral questions. When vast numbers of Catholics in the West have come to a view of reality that is directly counter to the view communicated by Jesus and the apostles and that is deeply embedded in the tradition and history of interpretation concerning the seriousness of sin and the very real possibility of ending up in hell rather than heaven, this has innumerable consequences for the life and mission of the Church. When the impression is common—as it is today—that almost everybody ends up in heaven and hardly anyone in hell, the seriousness of the call to holiness and the call to mission are significantly undermined. If the lists of sins that exclude people from the kingdom of God are not to be taken seriously (1 Cor 6:9–10; Gal 5:19–21; Eph 5:3–6), will not most people find it much easier to actually commit these sins?

Jean Galot, SJ, in commenting on von Balthasar's thesis, puts it this way: "It also removes all effectiveness from the warnings issued by Jesus, repeatedly expressed in the Gospels. We must take these evangelical warnings seriously....We cannot diminish the value of these warnings, formulated in an explicit manner; we must accept them in their truthfulness and seriously consider the dangers expressed. An empty hell could not be a threat and vigilance would become less necessary."[4]

If, in the last analysis, it does not really matter much if people come to explicit repentance, faith, baptism, and membership in the

Church, why bother with evangelization? Why make the effort and sacrifices entailed if, in the last analysis, everybody—or almost everybody—gets to heaven anyway? If anything ultimate and eternal is not really at stake, why bother? If there are no real consequences to believing or not believing and to obeying or not obeying, then why not pick and choose and do what one pleases?

There seem to be several reasons for the prevalence of this "virtual universalism." Certainly the speculative theology of Karl Rahner, his essays on the "anonymous Christian," and the aforementioned work of von Balthasar have made a contribution to this mentality. This is not to judge the merit or soundness of their work but merely to point out very unfortunate pastoral consequences with its popularization. But the pastoral/evangelistic strategy of Vatican II also seems to have played— perhaps unwittingly—a role. In the effort to renew the face of the Church so it could more clearly show forth the face of Christ to the world, the council consciously decided to "emphasize the positive" and did an excellent job of recontextualizing the deposit of faith in a more biblical, spiritual, and pastoral manner. This generally led to silence on some of the negative consequences of rejecting Christ and his message—namely, hell. One finds, to some degree, this silence concerning the consequences of rejecting Christ in the council documents themselves, but even more so in the postconciliar magisterial documents where hell is hardly mentioned—even in documents on evangelization where it could hardly not be mentioned if an integral biblical account was truly to be given.[5]

How does the Church understand, in its official teaching, the possibility of hell as a consequence for rejecting the gospel? And what implications does this have for evangelization? The *Catechism of the Catholic Church* is quite clear in its teaching on hell (see 1033–37), yet this teaching is very rarely adverted to.

While the overwhelming preponderance of scripture and theological tradition (including Augustine and Aquinas) holds that many, if not most, will in fact be lost, Cardinal Dulles identifies, in the *First Things* article previously referenced, a shift in the tradition that at least in part broadens the understanding of how God's grace for salvation is given beyond the visible limits of faith, baptism, and church membership. He indicates that this shift, beginning in the mid-twentieth century, is affirmed in the documents of Vatican II.

I think it is clear that a careful reading of the documents does evidence such a broadening, but with very important qualifications that are almost never adverted to. The most authoritative contemporary explication appears in *Lumen Gentium* 16.[6]

> Those who, through no fault of their own , do not know the Gospel of Christ or his Church, but who nevertheless seek God with a sincere heart, and moved by grace, try in their actions to do his will as they know it through the dictates of their conscience—those too may achieve eternal salvation....But very often, deceived by the Evil One, men have become vain in their reasonings, have exchanged the truth of God for a lie and served the world rather than the Creator (cf. Rom 1:21, 25). Or else, living and dying in this world without God, they are exposed to ultimate despair. Hence to procure the glory of God and the salvation of all these, the Church, mindful of the Lord's command, "preach the Gospel to every creature" (Mark 16:16) takes zealous care to foster the missions.

The council clearly acknowledges that God offers the possibility of salvation to people who have never heard the gospel. This is based on Romans 1:19–20, where scripture indicates that God reveals himself to everyone in some real way through creation, and on Romans 2:14–16, which indicates that the law of conscience is found in each person's heart, and, absent some additional revelation, will be the basis for condemnation or salvation. But there are very important qualifications that the council also makes.

First of all, it is those who "through no fault of their own" do not know the gospel who have the possibility of salvation. The implication seems to clearly be that people can be at fault for not hearing the gospel. One thinks of Paul's vigorous answer to the objection made in his time that perhaps so many Jews rejected Jesus because they really had not heard the good news:

> But I ask, have they not heard? Indeed they have; for
> "Their voice has gone out to all the earth,
>   and their words to the ends of the world."

Again I ask, did Israel not understand? First Moses says,
      "I will make you jealous of those who are not a nation;
        with a foolish nation I will make you angry."
Then Isaiah is so bold as to say,
      "I have been found by those who did not seek me;
        I have shown myself to those who did not ask for me."
But of Israel he says, "All day long I have held out my hands
    to a disobedient and contrary people." (Rom 10:18–21)

Second, salvation is possible for those who have not heard the gospel through no fault of their own, if they indeed "seek God with a sincere heart, and, moved by grace, try in their actions to do his will as they know it through the dictates of conscience." This seems to me to be a rather stiff requirement.

Third, the possibility of salvation does not exist in some neutral vacuum. There are opposing forces that seek to impel human beings to reject the light of conscience and prefer the works of darkness to the works of light, to search for self rather than God, and to do what satisfies the lust of the flesh, the lust of the eyes, and the pride of life rather than the will of God (1 John 2:15–17). In other words, "the world, the flesh, and the devil" are formidable obstacles to responding to the light and grace that God gives. The council acknowledges such with a rather striking reference to the downward spiral triggered by bad conscience that is described in the first chapter of Romans.

It is precisely these human beings without the gospel who very often yield to the deception of the devil, the allure of the flesh and the world, and the intellectual, moral, and spiritual confusion that comes from pride. Such people become subject to the just judgment of God—his wrath—since their choice against grace, against conscience, and against the light is without excuse (Rom 1:18–32).

And for those who hear and reject?

For it is indeed just of God to repay with affliction those who afflict you, and to give relief to the afflicted as well as to us, when the Lord Jesus is revealed from heaven with his mighty angels in flaming fire, inflicting vengeance on those who do not know God and on those who do not obey the gospel of our Lord Jesus. These will suffer the punishment

31

of eternal destruction, separated from the presence of the Lord and from the glory of his might, when he comes to be glorified by his saints and to be marveled at on that day among all who have believed, because our testimony to you was believed. (2 Thess 1:6–10)

It seems to me that a fair way of describing what has happened in Vatican II is a recovery of the range of scriptural teaching on salvation to allow for salvation outside of the visible confines of the Church and of explicit faith and sacramental baptism. A certain Catholic "fundamentalism" or "ecclesiocentrism" has been overcome, and God is allowed to be God.

On the other hand, it is important to see clearly how perilous the way to salvation remains for those who have not heard the gospel and are not members of the Church. I believe it is a huge mistake theologically and pastorally to move from the possibility of salvation apart from Christ and the Church to the probability or even presumption of such salvation.

Even with the necessary broadening of the tradition as evidenced in the passage from *Lumen Gentium* that we have been considering, the sobering words of Peter remain very apropos: "If it is hard for the righteous to be saved, what will become of the ungodly and the sinners?" (1 Pet 4:18).

While it may very well be that, in Cardinal Dulles's words, priests and theologians who give the impression that hell is a medieval superstition are doing "Satan's work," one thing is sure: they are not being faithful to the structure of reality as revealed to us in revelation, they are not accurately representing the actual teachings of Vatican II, they are seriously misleading people about the truth of our situation, and they are doctrinally undermining an important rationale for evangelization.

NOTES

1. In my article, which Cardinal Dulles cited in his presentation, I attempt to show how a misplaced compassion that *presumes* a happy outcome for suicides and aborted babies not only is untrue to revelation and the teaching of the Church, but actually can gravely damage people's lives. "Believing and Praying: The Power of Homilies," *Homiletic*

& *Pastoral Review* 104 (December 2003): 64–66. This article is also available online at www.renewalministries.net.

2. Cardinal Dulles has provided an excellent survey of what Scripture and Tradition teach about the reality of hell and the likelihood of people going there in an article that appeared in *First Things* 133 (May 2003): 36–41. My response to this article appeared in *First Things* 136 (October 2003): 3–4.

3. "Many Called, Few Chosen," in *Parochial and Plain Sermons: John Henry Newman* (San Francisco: Ignatius Press, 1987), 1118.

4. *Eschatology from the Second Vatican Council to Our Days*, www.clerus.org.

5. Pope Benedict XVI gave a commentary on Psalm 136 (137) at the general audience of November 30, 2005, in which, drawing on Augustine's commentary on the same psalm, he made the point that "people who are committed to peace and the good of the community" who are not Christians, and may not even have any explicit faith in God, can be saved. There was something of an uproar in the Italian press and radio about what was being interpreted as the pope declaring that one no longer needed to be a Christian to be saved; so much so that a professor at the Gregorian, Ilaria Morali, felt the need to respond in an interview that was published in two parts on Zenit (www.zenit.org), January 15 and 16, 2006, giving the scriptural and theological bases for the salvation of those who are not explicitly Christian. The focus, both in Pope Benedict XVI's original remarks and in Morali's further explanations, was on the possibility of nonbelievers being saved, but no mention was made of the strict conditions under which this is possible, nor the likelihood that (as *Lumen Gentium* 16 states) "very many" will not fulfill these conditions apart from the repentance and faith that comes from responding to the work of evangelization—the preaching of the gospel.

6. Other comments on this question in the council documents are found in *Ad Gentes Divinitus* 7 and *Gaudium et Spes* 22.

4

Reviving the Missionary Mandate

Richard John Neuhaus

Often we assume that Christianity always has been and will continue to be inherently missionary in character. Today, agreement with such an assumption cannot be assumed lightly.

In various Christian communities today, from Evangelical Protestant to Roman Catholic, there is a lively debate about "universalism." Universalism teaches that, in one way or another, all human beings will be eternally saved. If that is the case, it would seem to undercut any great sense of urgency about *missio ad gentes*: bringing the gospel to the nations—and to our own nation! Universalism is often thought to be a liberal or modernist position and it is vigorously opposed by conservatives, who, their critics say, seem to relish the prospect of watching multitudes burn eternally in hell. Such conservatives deny the charge, pointing to their earnestness in pursuing the missionary mandate precisely in order to rescue others from that doleful destiny.

In fact, the idea of universalism in one form or another has reappeared regularly in two thousand years of Christian history. The early fathers had a Greek name for the doctrine, *apocatastasis*, and by it they meant that ultimately all moral creatures—angels, men, and devils—would share in the grace of salvation. The doctrine is to be found in Clement of Alexandria, in Origen, and in St. Gregory of Nyssa. It was strongly attacked by St. Augustine, and this aspect of "Origenism" was condemned by the Council of Constantinople in 543. Nonetheless, universalism persists in the modern era, being defended by certain Anabaptists and Moravians, and by theologians in the tradition of the influential nineteenth-century Protestant liberal Friedrich Schleiermacher.

What might be called a modified version of universalism—that all people have at least the possibility of being saved, whether or not they have heard the gospel—is the official teaching of the Catholic Church today, and is embraced by many others as well. God does not deny to anyone the grace necessary for salvation. And that brings us to the question of the motives for evangelization. If the missionary enterprise is not driven by the imperative of rescuing souls from certain and everlasting perdition, the urgency of the enterprise, some say, would seem to be considerably relaxed.

Countering Confusions

That is among the issues addressed by Pope John Paul II in his eighth encyclical, *Redemptoris Missio* (Mission of the Redeemer). The pope believed that many Catholics are confused about the reason for missions, and that confusion has everything to do with the marked decline in devotion to the missionary effort.

Since Catholics are not the only ones confused on this point, it may be that the encyclical can be an ecumenical "teaching moment" that contributes to a broader understanding of Christian mission and evangelization in the third millennium. With respect to missions, John Paul II wrote in *Redemptoris Missio*, "There is an undeniable negative tendency, and the present document is meant to help overcome it" (2). He cited Pope Paul VI, who pointed to "the lack of fervor which is all the more serious because it comes from within. It is manifested in fatigue, disenchantment, compromises, lack of interest, and above all lack of joy and hope" (36).*

Those are just the symptoms, John Paul suggested. The causes are cultural and, mainly, theological. What he calls the negative tendency "is based on incorrect theological perspectives and is characterized by

---

*Quotations by other people and references to other documents all occur within *Redemptoris Missio*. The section numbers throughout refer only to that encyclical.

a religious relativism which leads to the belief that 'one religion is as good as another'" (36). He thinks it an "insidious" factor that some people invoke the teaching of the Second Vatican Council in order to justify indifference to evangelization.

Early on in *Redemptoris Missio,* John Paul laid out the questions to which he proposed answers.

> [As] a result of the changes which have taken place in modern times and the spread of new theological ideas, some people wonder: Is missionary work among non-Christians still relevant? Has it not been replaced by interreligious dialogue? Is not human development an adequate goal of the Church's mission? Does not respect for conscience and for freedom exclude all efforts at conversion? Is it not possible to attain salvation in any religion? Why then should there be missionary activity? (4)

A Universal Possibility of Salvation

John Paul repeatedly affirmed the statement of Vatican II's *Gaudium et Spes* that "we are obliged to hold that the Holy Spirit offers everyone the possibility of sharing in the paschal mystery in a manner known to God" (6). He insisted, however, that that teaching in no way undercuts the uniqueness and universal significance of God's self-revelation in Jesus Christ. On the contrary, the universal possibility of salvation is premised upon the uniqueness of the Christian truth. Put differently, the claim that salvation is possible for everyone, including non-Christians, is inseparable from Jesus Christ, who is "the way, the truth, and the life" to whom Christians bear witness.

John Paul said with Peter, "There is salvation in no one else, for there is no other name under heaven given among mortals by which we must be saved" (Acts 4:12). The point is that those who are saved without knowing the name of Christ are nonetheless saved by Christ. In *Redemptoris Missio,* the pope stated it this way: "No one, therefore, can enter into communion with God except through Christ, by the working of the Holy Spirit. Christ's one, universal mediation...is the way established by God himself....Although participated forms of mediation of different kinds and degrees [through other religions] are not excluded, they acquire meaning and value only from Christ's own mediation, and they cannot be understood as parallel or complementary to his" (5). Other religious ways may be salvific only because they participate, albeit unknowingly, in the salvation worked by the One who is the Way.

Toward an Ultimate Unity

Thus, despite the failures of Christians and non-Christians alike, God's plan is "to unite all things in Christ, things in heaven and things on earth" (Eph 1:10). In that plan, the Church is the sacrament of salvation, and here John Paul cited *Lumen Gentium* of Vatican II: "To this catholic unity of the people of God, therefore...all are called, and they belong to it, or are ordered to it in various ways, whether they be Catholic faithful or others who believe in Christ or finally all people everywhere who by the grace of God are called to salvation" (9).

He went on to comment, "But it is clear that today, as in the past, many people do not have an opportunity to come to know or accept the Gospel revelation or to enter the Church....For such people, salvation in Christ is accessible by virtue of a grace which, while having a mysterious relationship to the Church, does not make them formally part of the Church" (10). Such universally available grace is not something natural to the human condition apart from Christ. "This grace comes from Christ; it is the result of his sacrifice and is communicated by the Holy Spirit" (10).

"It is necessary," said the pope, "to keep these truths together, namely, the real possibility of salvation in Christ for all mankind and the necessity of the Church for salvation. Both these truths help us to understand the one mystery of salvation, so that we can come to know God's mercy and our own responsibility" (9). Most Catholics and Protestants may readily agree that it is necessary to keep those truths together, but it is not always easy.

The fact is that many Christians today are puzzled, even embarrassed, by the heroic stories of missionaries of the past who braved unspeakable persecutions and even martyrdom in carrying out the missionary mandate to the nations. According to a good many contemporary theologians, it used to be that the "ordinary" means of salvation was through Christ and his Church, while allowance was made for "extraordinary" means in the case of those who never had a chance to hear the gospel. But now, some are saying, the situation has been reversed; the ordinary has become the extraordinary, and the extraordinary the ordinary.

Well aware of that way of thinking, John Paul nonetheless declared: "The mission of Christ the redeemer, which is entrusted to the Church, is still very far from completion. As the second millennium after Christ's coming draws to an end, an overall view of the human race shows that this mission is still only beginning and that we must commit ourselves wholeheartedly to its service" (1). His intention is to "relaunch the mission *ad gentes*." "Christian hope sustains us in committing ourselves fully to the new evangelization and to the worldwide mission" (86). Then this vision: "As the third millennium of the redemption draws near, God is preparing a great springtime for Christianity, and we can already see its first signs" (86).

Six Reasons

What possible reason, what urgently compelling reason, can motivate Christians to commit themselves wholeheartedly to such evangelization? If in God's plan salvation is already available to all— available through Christ, to be sure—what is the irresistible incitement to give oneself to the missionary endeavor? It is fine for the pope to say that "missionary activity represents the greatest challenge for the Church today" (40), but why, finally, should Christians care about the mission *ad gentes*—or why should we care as much as John Paul so earnestly wanted us to care?

The reasons are not set out systematically, but one can extract from *Redemptoris Missio* six distinct, although not separable, arguments for commitment to the evangelization of the world. Not necessarily in order of importance, the six arguments are these: the nature and vitality of the Church; love of neighbor; duty to neighbor; Christian unity;

obedience to the mission of Christ, and the concern of Christians for their own salvation.

"In the Church's history," John Paul wrote, "missionary drive has always been a sign of vitality, just as its lessening is a sign of a crisis of faith" (2). "Missionary activity," he contended, "renews the Church, revitalizes faith and Christian identity, and offers fresh enthusiasm and new incentive. Faith is strengthened when it is given to others!" (2). What the pope said about the vitality of the Church would seem to be historically and psychologically undeniable. Beyond that, he employed elaborate biblical support in arguing that it is the very nature of the Church to be missionary. "The preaching of the early Church was centered on the proclamation of Jesus Christ, with whom the kingdom was identified" (16). Although John Paul did not put it quite this way, the implication is that, without missionary commitment, the continuity between the contemporary Church and the New Testament Church is obscured, perhaps even thrown into question.

In addition to the vitality and nature of the Church, the pope argued from the second of what Jesus called the great commandments, love for neighbor. "What moves me even more strongly to proclaim the urgency of missionary evangelization is the fact that it is the primary service that the Church can render to every individual and to all humanity," he wrote (2). It is both the primary service and the utterly distinctive service. Other institutions can do many of the good things done by the Church, but only the Church proclaims the fullness of God's revelation in Christ. If the Church does not do that, nobody else will. "Every form of the Spirit's presence is to be welcomed with respect and gratitude, but the discernment of this presence is the responsibility of the Church, to which Christ gave his Spirit in order to guide her into all truth (cf. John 16)" (29). According to John Paul, for Christians not to do all they can to propose to others this fullness of life in Christ is, quite simply, to violate the law of love.

Third, and obviously related, is duty to the neighbor. "No believer in Christ, no institution of the Church, can avoid this supreme duty: to proclaim Christ to all peoples," said the pope (3). "Faith demands a free adherence on the part of man, but at the same time faith must also be offered to him" (8). He again quoted Paul VI: "The multitudes have the right to know the riches of the mystery of Christ—riches in which we believe that the whole of humanity can find, in unsuspected fullness, everything that it is gropingly searching for concerning God, man and his destiny, life and death, and truth" (8). To abdicate the missionary task, then, is to deny human beings their rights. Put differently, they have "a right to know," so that they might have an opportunity to believe.

And Ecumenism

The fourth reason for recommitment to the mission *ad gentes* may strike some as a bit odd. "The missionary thrust," the pope said in the beginning of the encyclical, "therefore belongs to the very nature of the Christian life and is also the inspiration behind ecumenism: 'That they may all be one...so that the world may believe that you have sent me' (John 17:21)" (1). Much later he returned to the question of Christian unity. Concern for mission, he wrote, "will serve as a motivation and stimulus for a renewed commitment to ecumenism" (50). This is because divisions among Christians "weaken their witness" to the world, and because reconciliation among Christians is itself a "sign of the work of God" that Christians proclaim. So, commitment to ecumenism is for the sake of mission, and a renewed commitment to mission requires commitment to ecumenism.

One notes in passing that ecumenism in *Redemptoris Missio* appears to be limited to those churches with which the Catholic Church "is engaged in dialogue." The aggressively missionary Evangelicals and Pentecostals—and here the pope surely had Latin America in mind— are viewed as a "threat," and he intimated that the Catholic Church and its dialogue partners should join in opposing them. This apparently truncated ecumenical vision is tactically understandable, but it perhaps underestimates the degree to which cooperation with these groups is growing, as witness the project "Evangelicals and Catholics Together" in this country.

The fifth argument—which John Paul said is the most fundamental—is that mission is what God has done and is doing in Christ. "God has revealed to mankind who he is. This definitive self-revelation of God is the fundamental reason why the Church is missionary by her very nature" (5). It is a question of letting Christ do his work. "He carries out his mission through the Church" (9). The missionary mandate is a matter of obedience to Christ.

The pope cited the words of Jesus in John 20:21: "As the Father has sent me, even so I send you." The Good Shepherd searches out the lost and gives his life for the sheep (John 10), and therefore "those who have the missionary spirit share Christ's burning love for souls" (89). In short, for people who would be disciples of Christ the missionary mandate is not optional, for the only Christ who can be known is the Christ who declares his intention to be in continuing mission through his disciples.

Sixth and finally, the pope's answer to the question "Why evangelization?" comes back to its being a matter of salvation—except the salvation in question is not just that of non-Christians as that of Christians. "Mission is an issue of faith," he wrote, "an accurate indicator of our faith in Christ and his love for us" (11). Or again, "Why mission? Because to us, as to St. Paul, 'this grace was given to preach to the gentiles the unsearchable riches of Christ' (Eph 3:8)" (11). Mission is required by "the profound demands of God's life within us."

"Those who are incorporated in the Catholic Church ought to sense their privilege and for that reason their greater obligation of bearing witness to the faith" (11). Once more quoting *Lumen Gentium*, he wrote: "They owe their distinguished status not to their own merits, but to Christ's special grace; and if they fail to respond to this grace in thought, word, and deed, not only will they not be saved, they will be judged more severely" (11). So it turns out that salvation is at stake after all—the salvation of those who are Christians.

Truth Claims and Threats

These are the six reasons for the mission *ad gentes* that seem to emerge from a close reading of *Redemptoris Missio*. In this encyclical, John Paul was not simply issuing a pronouncement, he was making an argument. His argument challenges deeply entrenched fears about Christian "triumphalism," "cultural imperialism," and the such. It does not sit well with cultural prohibitions against proselytizing, and it potentially offends regnant notions of tolerance and pluralism. The argument is, in sum, profoundly countercultural. Catholics and non-

Catholics who would engage the argument, however, must engage it at its heart, namely, that the truth claims of the Christian gospel leave Christians no choice but to be people in mission to others.

Those who are not Christians may, understandably, be inclined to view any revival of the missionary mandate as threatening or as a matter of indifference, of interest only to Christians. To those who view it as threatening, John Paul adamantly insisted that complete religious freedom and the rejection of every form of coercion is integral to the gospel. "The Church imposes nothing; she only proposes" (39).

Those, on the other hand, who think the question of evangelization is purely an internal Christian concern fail to appreciate the powerful bearing that this question has on the attitude of 2.2 billion Christians toward world history, and, consequently, on the shaping of the third millennium. Whether the argument of *Redemptoris Missio* is consigned to the dusty shelves reserved for official ecclesiastical documents or is taken up by the Christians of our time will have an enormous bearing on the future.

Had I not been limited by the confines of a short article, I might have explored the many writings of Cardinal Ratzinger, now Pope Benedict XVI, on the reasons why the cause of evangelization has been weakened in recent decades, and how it might be renewed. But, in pondering those writings, I was struck by how marvelously they converge with the teaching of *Redemptoris Missio*. There is no surprise in that, for there was the most remarkable collaboration between John Paul II and Cardinal Ratzinger, and Pope Benedict has repeatedly said that it is the great goal of his pontificate to advance the vision of his venerable predecessor.

I earnestly hope that this will be a *Redemptoris Missio* age, in joyful obedience to the command of Christ to go into all the world—all the neighborhoods, all the homes, all the workplaces—to share the good news of salvation, the good news of God's immeasurable love.

Evangelizing Our Culture

> *Francis Cardinal George, OMI*

The culture in which we evangelize is also the object of our evangelizing efforts. Why should that be so? The culture in which we evangelize itself needs to be evangelized because evangelizing means bringing people to faith in Jesus Christ within his body the Church, where they can get to know him as he truly is and experience his action in scripture and the sacraments, both of which are expressions of his love. Evangelizing means, then, bringing individuals and everything they are to Jesus Christ. Of course, they are more than individuals. What they are, beyond isolated individuals, is sometimes summarized as their culture. Culture can be said to be the nonbiological inheritance that creates our life. Culture, like faith itself, shapes our very lives. Both culture and faith tell us how to behave and what to believe. Both give us norms for acting and for thinking and for loving. Bringing people, therefore, to know and love and accept Christ in the Church is easier or harder, depending upon what their culture tells them is good to know and to love and to accept.[1]

Recognizing this importance of culture's interaction with faith, an importance underscored for the first time in the magisterium of the Church by the Second Vatican Council, Pope Paul VI wrote that the split between gospel and culture is the drama of our times. He added immediately, however, that it was the drama of other ages as well, because the Catholic faith never fits perfectly into any human culture. "Therefore," Paul VI added, "every effort must be made to ensure a full evangelization of culture or, more correctly, of cultures. They have to be regenerated by an encounter with the gospel. But this encounter will not take place if the gospel is not proclaimed."[2] The dialogue between faith and culture is as old as the history of God's self-revelation and the human response to it in faith. This dialogue between faith and culture is called the "inculturation of the faith." It means that a particular culture's symbols, institutions, and values become vehicles for expressing the universal faith. Missiologists invented the term *inculturation* as a way of rooting the dialogue between faith and culture in the mystery of the incarnation of the Son of God. Just as the Word of God became man, the faith of the Church becomes Nigerian, Chinese, or American—as Nigerians, Chinese, and Americans come to know, love, and accept Christ. Pope John Paul II, as he went around the world, always said, "In you Christ has become Chinese or Nigerian or Filipino," and in us, therefore, Christ has become American. How does this happen?[3]

Between a transcendent gift of faith and an immanent construction of culture there will always be some tension, as I remarked above. Sometimes a given culture will not possess the resources for expressing the faith in all its fullness. A culture might be unable to make sense of God's self-revelation, unable to understand a merciful Father, an obedient Son, and a self-effacing Spirit. Beyond the inevitable tensions that arise when a culture is stretched to express the Catholic faith, more positive resistance might develop. A culture can resist the faith as a sinner resists grace. Individuals convert, so must cultures be transformed. But the culture might enshrine customs opposed to living according to the gospel: polygamy, ritual murder, sexual promiscuity, abortion, and exploitative business practices. When believers recognize demonic elements in their culture and work to diminish or eradicate them, the dialogue between faith and culture turns into the evangelization of culture. Culture is the object of our evangelization and not just the sea in which we swim. To form gospel-shaped people, the Church must work to create gospel-friendly cultures.

The faith that demands that culture change is sometimes called countercultural. I think the adjective can be unfortunate, because it leads believers to see themselves on one side and their culture on another. Our culture is as much in us as we are in it. Religious critics of the culture can imagine a bad system opposed by good people. But that distinction is too easy. If our social system and culture are at least in part evangelically deficient or even corrupt, so are we all. The evangelizer begins by taking responsibility for the culture that has to be evangelized. But separating the good from the bad in a culture's values and way of life, its institutional patterns, its goals and accomplishments demands a principle of discernment. What is good and what is bad? And when the Catholic evangelizer looks for such a principle, he or she reaches for the gospel as interpreted by the faith of the Church. The Church tells us that our culture, despite its deficiencies and the positive obstacles it might place to belief, finally, is lovable.

The Catholic Church teaches that grace builds on nature, because human nature, while wounded by sin, is not hopelessly corrupt. As grace builds on nature, so faith builds on culture, which is second nature. Culture is terribly damaged by human sinfulness, but seldom is it hopelessly corrupt. A culture is a field that offers plants from native seeds for grafting onto the tree of the universal faith. Pope John Paul II, in his various visits to peoples around the world, always tried to help them see the seeds of the word in any culture. He found the seed of God's word in his first visit as pope to the United States in 1979, when he saw the many different peoples that came together to form this country. He looked out at a vast field of people on the shore of Lake Michigan in Chicago and he recalled St. Paul's description of the Church: "We, though many, are one people in Christ" (see 1 Cor 12:12). While cultural unity is very different from the communion of faith, nonetheless, there is something analogous in our experience of the American enterprise that enables us to catch a glimpse of the unity and the diversity of the Catholic communion.

We must do what John Paul II did—search for the seeds of what is generally good—so that we can then criticize and transform and evangelize what is truly demonic. In an evangelized culture, turns of phrase and cherished customs, habitual attitudes and daily activities, serve to remind people of the gospel of Christ. Pope John Paul II said many times that faith must become culture. "The faith that has not become culture," the pope explained, "is not fully received, not entirely thought through, not faithfully lived."[4] Faith is not true to its own nature unless it transforms everything in a particular culture. Faith becomes culture, however, only as a culture is open to the ultimate truth about human nature and human destiny. And so we must now turn to look at our own American culture.

45

The Ways in Which American Culture Resists Catholicism

While the Church in the United States enjoys a certain institutional freedom, now more and more menaced, she exists in a culture that in often surprising ways resists Catholicism. Are there clues then to the American pattern of resistance to Catholic faith? Are there indicators that must be taken into account when we look at obstacles to evangelizing our culture and, therefore, our people?

Perhaps Americans have greater difficulty than others in understanding their own culture. The United States, while too small to be *the* world, is big enough to be *a* world. Unlike the people of Denmark or Zimbabwe or Uruguay, Americans can interpret people elsewhere only in terms of American experience, and this infuriates other peoples more than we often imagine. Since American popular culture influences the world, we can be easily led into thinking that all peoples are more like us than, in fact, they are. In order to safeguard a national unity that crosses great distances created from peoples of many races, national origins, religions, and cultures, Americans often relegate differences to the private sphere, explaining that all peoples are really alike, at least under the skin. This is done to preserve our own unity and also to justify a kind of American messianism around the world. Americans' awareness of their own cultural peculiarity is suppressed by American culture itself.

While we have a particular problem in analyzing our own culture, however, the evangelizer anywhere is hard put to analyze his or her own culture. It's too much part of himself or herself. Cultural analysis must include, therefore, a way of uncovering the meaning and the values implicit in the people's behavior. This analysis includes the historical influences in a society and a notion about how cultures interact, develop, and are transmitted. I came to this question from my own experience as vicar general of the Oblates of Mary Immaculate, going from country to country and listening to missionaries—often foreign— asking whether we were sure that we were just transmitting the gospel of Jesus Christ rather than also imposing our own culture from France, the United States, or Canada.

This is a question that missionaries have been asking for a hundred years. They've developed certain modes of analysis to help them

46

understand the culture that they are addressing and evangelizing and to respect it so that they do not propose anything other than the faith itself to the people to whom they are sent. From cultural anthropology, the evangelizer learns methods of questioning that tease out meanings and values hidden in collective behavior. Let's take, for example, the family picnic in the United States on the Fourth of July. A cultural anthropologist preparing to "evangelize" American picnickers begins with questions: *Who are they?* People related by blood and marriage. *What are they doing?* Eating hot dogs, playing a ball game, talking. *When are they doing it?* On a summer day. *Where are they doing it?* In the open air. *How are they doing it?* Some cooking, some cleaning, some organizing games, but all cooperating. *And what kind of activity is this picnic really?* A family coming together to relax in the context of a larger civic holiday. Each of these questions enables the evangelizer to note the forms by which a culture organizes itself on this occasion.

But the more important questions remain to be asked: *Why* is the family celebrating? *Why?* Because that's the final question for any evangelizer trying to understand the situation. *We* have an answer to that question from faith, but one must ask what the answer from culture is. On one level "why" is answered functionally. The family eats hot dogs in order to satisfy their hunger without preparing an elaborate meal. The family plays games in order to exercise. The family spends time together because they love each other. But if the evangelizer continues to question why a whole nation engages in this kind of behavior on the fourth day of the month of July each year, a deeper level of meaning unfolds. The story of the Fourth of July in the year 1776 is told. Bits of multicolored bunting are displayed, and the evangelizer recognizes the flag of the country. Hot dogs are not just energy resources but typical food of the country. The ball games are described as the country's national pastime. Participating in the event is a way of reaffirming values: nationality, independence, and personal freedom. The event itself is a symbol of the family's participation in the life and purposes of the nation. It is important to go into this kind of analysis in trying to understand why people are who they are. In short, the family picnic displays meanings and values that define the cultural context and are taken, for the most part, for granted by people who live all their time in that culture.

These "why" questions need to be pressed until the evangelizer recognizes an order of importance, a hierarchy, among the meanings and values discovered in the culture that he or she is evangelizing. Understanding a culture's distinctive character indicates at what points an evangelizer must foster that culture's dialogue with universal Catholic faith.

Besides cultural anthropology and the questions it gives us, we can look at historical analysis to try to understand our own or any other culture. Observation and questioning uncover meanings and values, but studying the group's history explains why a culture transmits only certain meanings and cherishes particular values more than others. History explains the *hierarchy* of values. In the case of the United States, our culture's historical roots are traced to the Pilgrims and the English Puritan dissenters, to the American Enlightenment, to the founders of the republic who created the forms of American democracy, and to the activists and pragmatists of the last three and a half centuries whose work generated economic growth. Each of these strengths, sometimes existing in the same historical personage, has interacted with the others to create the distinctive system of values and meanings that is American culture.

No matter what our culture's roots, we recognize that we live now in a society no longer integrated by religious faith. Most Americans might believe in some sort of god, but faith is compartmentalized, meaning that it is unrelated to much of contemporary experience and life. The practice of a religious faith is a "hobby," something to do in your spare time on a weekend, but not something to bring into the rest of your life. And if it is so brought in, it will be immediately questioned.

Returning momentarily to the historical roots of our culture, Puritanism would seem to have lost the most ground in a secularized society. Yet attitudes and values can endure even when separated from the historical movements that gave them birth. I would argue that America is different from other modern secular societies because it is a secularized Puritan society, rather than a culture that has simply replaced the Puritan influence with something else. To speak of Puritan attitudes and habits, meanings and values, surviving in this society may seem strange. But the conflict can hide a deeper continuity. The Puritan conversion narratives of colonial Massachusetts show a pattern that remains familiar today. This is a pattern of behavior that becomes very clear in the detailed diaries that the early colonialists kept. Why did they keep them?

Briefly, the answer to this question is that, in Puritan New England, proof of internal conversion to Christ was required to be admitted to church membership. The candidate for membership testified before the local congregation's representatives to the workings of grace in his or her soul. The congregation, for its part, had to listen very carefully and respectfully to this recital of personal religious experience. Dependent upon the successful acceptance of this person's conversion, he or she would be not only a member of the church but also, in many places, a member of society. Furthermore, attention to feelings was of particular importance in establishing one's right to belong. Personal experience and its public recital thus became the rhetoric of American identity. Americans claim a right to belong by reason of the personal experience that they choose to disclose and that demands the respect of others who listen to it. Phenomena as diverse as civil rights, client-centered therapies, and talk shows find legitimation in this cultural pattern. Beyond a local congregation, Puritans also belonged to the New Israel, the kingdom of God in a new land in America. The Puritan's Sabbath was a symbol of Christ's entrance into his Father's kingdom after the work of redemption. And weekly Sabbath observance made the American Puritan community the church in a new and purified form, without the baggage of the Catholic history that encumbered even Protestant lands in once-Catholic Europe.

The United States has no "medieval" memories. To the Puritans, America was a new dispensation. Here the kingdom of God was at hand and God's coming was presaged in a series of revivals, beginning with the Great Awakening of the 1740s and renewed periodically to this day. When, in the last century, the nation's purpose became the spread of democracy rather than the spread of the gospel, Americans still thought of their land as a light to other nations and themselves as people with a mission. American public discourse remains millennialist. Puritan eschatology is echoed in predictions of nuclear holocaust or ecological disaster. The end is always near and we must change our ways—because even if we no longer believe in an angry God, the wounded earth will punish us.

The secularization of Puritan rhetoric and behavior began early. Alexis de Tocqueville, who visited the United States early in the nineteenth century to see how democratic structures were influencing character development here, noted that Americans were individualists. Is this a help or hindrance to the Catholic evangelizer? Like many cultural phenomena, individualism is evangelically ambiguous. On the one hand, if it means that each person is regarded as unique and even sacred, that persons are valuable because they have either experienced justification by God's grace or, more recently, by declaring themselves estimable, individualism can be fertile soil for planting the Catholic faith. On the other hand, whatever merits it might possess as a foundation for civic life, individualism is an unreliable base for Catholic ecclesial communion.

De Tocqueville discovered that the notion of the voluntary association was a logical corollary to individualism in America. The voluntary association bridged the gap between the individual self and the larger society. American individuals did not isolate themselves. They formed and joined groups for social purposes, just as Puritan believers, individually converted, joined the local congregation. Voluntary associations conformed also to the Enlightenment vision of rational individuals forming a social contract, respecting the rights of each but providing common security and the means for all to advance economically and politically. Americans, therefore, belong to all kinds of voluntary associations: the Red Cross, Green Peace, the Moose and the Elks, the ACLU, the Holy Name Society, a parent-teacher association, and so on. Americans have a right to belong provided only that they do so freely and have the experience that the rules demand for membership.

This brings us back to the reason why individualism is an unreliable basis for Catholic ecclesial communion. This deeply ingrained pattern of individualism and voluntary association is a very inadequate analog for the Catholic self-understanding of the Church as a hierarchical and participatory communion. American culture understands basically two ways of being religious: liberal and evangelical. This distinction crosses all the now-historical denominational boundaries. How do these two differ?

To oversimplify to the point of distortion, liberal religion treats God as an ideal, a goal expressing all that is best in human experience, while the real agents of change in the world are human persons. Religious language is important poetry, agnostic about who God is but expressive of our experience of wholeness. The traditional sacraments are signs of our own interior dispositions and intentions. Worship might be structured, but at its heart, religion is ethical and its social agenda is central.

By contrast, and again to indulge in gross simplification, Evangelicals have a keen sense of God's agency. God is real, independent, powerful, active. Evangelicals know God from their emotional experience of prayer and from the reading of God's holy word. Religious language, at least among fundamentalists, is literal, and the Bible is often read much like a newspaper. Sacraments at best are signs of the interior faith that is given us before we receive them. The social agenda tends to be peripheral because God will change things at the beginning of the millennium, the apocalyptic rapture, or some other moment we can only wait for.

This split in the American Calvinist religious heritage occurred in the last century during the controversies over Darwin's theory of the evolution of species and the legitimacy of historical-critical approaches to Bible study. They continued throughout that century and continue into the present one. Some denominational lines were redrawn on the basis of liberal and evangelical tendencies. Lost in this redrawing is the truly Catholic sense of the Church as mediator of God's life and teacher of his truth. Also lost is the understanding of the Church as a body that one is joined to by baptism in order to be converted, not a voluntary association one chooses to be part of. Many American Catholics no longer belong to subcultures that for many decades buttressed Catholic identity while permitting interaction with society in general. The subcultures that built our great institutions—parochial schools and Catholic hospitals and charities—are disappearing, and thus no longer foster the resources needed to express the Catholic faith.

Threats to the Church's Evangelical Freedom

If we look first to our culture's institutional life and then at the values we've spoken about, we can understand why the Church's mission to evangelize is now, I believe, threatened externally by an erosion of our institutional freedom. In the United States we tend generally to speak about faith/culture differences as if they were church/state differences. We institutionalize the realities and movements because it is easier to speak about them in that way and because the language of

constitutional law and constitutional process is the only universal public language in our culture. The Church's mission to evangelize is now
faced with a certain loss of institutional freedom. This threat is occa-
sioned most clearly by the scandal of the sexual abuse of minors by
some priests and the failure of adequate oversight by some bishops.
This development has brought about a more overt expression of the
anti-Catholicism that has always marked American culture, as I've tried
to analyze it. In this context, courts and legislatures are more ready not
only to restrict publicly the freedom of the Church but also to interfere in the internal government of the Church in ways that are new to
our American experience. Our freedom to govern ourselves is being
diminished. The Church's mission to evangelize is further weakened by
her inability to shape a public conversation that would enable people
to understand the gospel and the demands of Christian discipleship in
the Church. And in our inability to shape that public conversation,
we've become ever more vulnerable to institutional interference.

Interference in the government of the Church arises also because
of the interpretation of the first amendment that has become part of
the jurisprudence of the Supreme Court in the last half-century. One
could argue, and the argument has been made in great detail elsewhere
by others, that religion is now constitutionally protected as a form of
self-expression, but not as religion itself. The guarantees that we
believe the First Amendment provided are now eroded. Our public
conversation speaks easily only of individual rights, and with the abso-
lutizing of individual rights, we cannot easily give voice to considera-
tions of the common good. Matters that should fall outside the purview
of law in a constitutional democracy with a limited government (for
example, the nature of marriage, the very nature of life, the nature even
of faith itself) are now determined by courts designed only to protect
individual rights. The increasingly oppressive legal system and the
bureaucratic apparatus of the State are abetted by a media industry that
selects for publication only facts that generate stories it wants to tell.
The public conversation about the political, legal, and economic system is based not on analysis but on the generation of conflicts between
individuals and interest groups.

The gospel calls us to receive freedom as a gift from God (see Eph
5:13) and to exercise that freedom faithfully, that is, "oriented towards
the goods of marriage and the flourishing of family life."[5] Hence,

Christ's faithful are called by the gospel to make choices that are worthy of the vocation that they've received in Christ. But in our culture, that is often regarded as an oppressive demand, and the Church, which voices those demands publicly, is seen as an enemy of personal freedom and even a cause of social violence. The public conversation in the United States is often an exercise in manipulation and always inadequate to the realities of both the country and the world, let alone to the mysteries of the Catholic faith. This conversation fundamentally distorts Catholicism and any other institution regarded as antithetical to the secular individualist ethos. Our freedom, therefore, to preach the gospel today is much diminished both personally and institutionally.

The diminishing of Catholic freedom to convert others is sometime justified by a belief that religious pluralism protects freedom itself. American freedom is complex and it is not fair to reduce American culture to consumerism, hedonism, selfish individualism, and oppression of minority groups. These vices, like American virtues, are part of larger historical developments in our culture. In the end, tabulating collective strengths and weaknesses, virtues and vices, successes and failures, can distract from the more fundamental question: "Does this culture now provide a sound context for human life or does it stifle the human experience?"

This question is also implicit in contemporary discussions about the end of history. On the one hand, some argue that our culture has universal significance and values. Modern science, liberalism, separation of civil society and state or church and state, the rule of law, the welfare state, democracy, "universal" conventions, declarations, and bills of rights are viewed as Western inventions that belong to specific periods of Western history, but they have now spread and imposed themselves in other parts of the world with the claim that they have universal value. On the other hand, others argue that, in the emerging world of ethnic conflict and civilizational clash, Western belief in the universality of Western culture is false, immoral, and dangerous. Does an evangelizer have to decide which of these positions is correct? Pared down for my purpose here, I would put the matter as follows: Suppose that the universality of Western institutions is an illusion and that Western culture is one among many cultures. We might still argue that it is the best, or, at least, that it is ours and that we must do what we can to preserve it and, if possible, to extend it. This brings us back to the fundamental question for those of us engaged in evangelizing our culture: Does the culture now provide some context for human life or does it stifle the human spirit? And as always, the answer is both yes and no. Pope John Paul II, when he went around speaking to the various peoples of the world, pointed out that an evangelizer of culture brings out evils that are truly there, but only to show the power of God's Word to heal and uplift, to unify and to bind with love.

A Five-Point Program for Evangelizing the Culture in Which We Live

We have looked at the obstacles hindering the Church's evangelizing the culture in which we live. It remains to ask, how can we overcome them? In this concluding section, I will outline a program for evangelizing American culture. This program, of course, begins, continues, and ends with love for the people and for the culture that makes them who they are. The people whom God calls to form Christ's Body are constantly in an evangelizer's prayer. Prayer itself, an activity with no immediately productive goal, evangelizes culture by introducing a rhythm of life that opens daily life to the transcendent. In a society driven by short-term goals, the inner discipline needed to live prayerfully day-by-day creates an alternative sense of time. Praying, as a habit, is the beginning for evangelizing our culture.

Second, the evangelizer of culture will look for the places where significant conversations take place, where the gospel might be proclaimed. A culture is a communications network and the gospel is a message. The evangelizer needs to be present in most places where the messages that form the culture are created and transmitted. That's why the Church is so interested in modern media, calling them the new Areopagus, the place where the world meets, as St. Paul met the people of Athens and Corinth in his time. It's why the Holy See belongs to the United Nations and regularly tries to shape discussions there. It's why I believe we should perhaps try to convert taxi drivers and bartenders, because their conversations shape people often when they are in a somewhat confessional mode. The Word of God could be inserted if people were trained to evangelize as they drive and as they serve.

Third, American evangelizers need to enlarge their culture's appreciation of the truth-attaining capacity of human reason. John Paul II's 1998 encyclical, *Fides et Ratio*, is a plea for restoring our confidence in human reason. He argues that reason is diminished when it is reduced to a calculating means for achieving individual ends or when it must be reduced to the methodology of the natural sciences of physics, biology, and chemistry. We need to expand the scope of reason beyond this instrumentalist conception in order to restore its capacity for attaining knowledge of ultimate truth regarding God, humanity, and the world.

Fourth, the dominant culture in the United States privileges voluntary relationships to the detriment of others, and hence the evangelizer must work to strengthen relations that are given rather than chosen: family, race, linguistic group, the land and nation itself as our home rather than a willed messianic project. Within the context of these relationships, the Church's gift of ecclesial communion with the source of life and the love of Father, Son, and Holy Spirit becomes culturally possible. American culture reduces the Church to a voluntary association and treats the nation itself the same way. American cultural myths, by reason of our history, are inevitably voluntaristic. We are a people of choice rather than our blood. One can choose to become American in a way that one cannot become Japanese, Navajo, or Arab. The melting-pot myth has enabled the United States to welcome almost anyone and everyone, at least in principle. Its inclusivity can serve the gospel's universalism. It cannot, however, be allowed to destroy the public legitimacy of nonvoluntary relationships and communities, as has happened to a great extent to marriage and now also in the case of the Church. The Catholic evangelizer in the United States will cherish and strengthen the relationships that faith tells us we have no right to "unchoose."

Fifth, evangelizing American culture means purifying our sense of mission. Catholics believe that groups do play roles in salvation history. But a collective vocation within God's call to everyone is different from the Puritans' notion of their particular covenant with the Lord. Since forming our national purpose in the light of God's plan for all people means listening to a source of truth not limited by American experience, our cultural resources are not sufficient; they fail us. We have in American culture resources for reexpressing evangelical freedom. Freedom is our prime cultural value, or has been until security began to take its place several years ago. We have resources for reexpressing evangelical justice, because justice is another cultural value. Even when we recognize the deficiencies of our theories of justice worked out in terms of individual equality, justice nonetheless remains a public imperative. The Church can figure in conversations around justice and help change institutions and structures.

Yet there are few public resources in our culture for reexpressing evangelical truth, because religious truth is no longer a public virtue. Any truth not immediately verifiable in observation or through the methodologies of the hard sciences becomes private opinion. The public authority, the government, while it must protect individual freedom and foster justice, cannot teach truth. But the Church can. And this claim to teach truth is truly countercultural. It explains why anti-Catholicism is a socially and intellectually respectable prejudice among much of the cultural elite in this country. Since the culture is too narrow for gospel truth, Catholic evangelizers want to enlarge it. We have the methods of analysis in cultural anthropology and in history and we have concern for institutions and for values, all of which must be converted so that individuals, once converted themselves through God's grace, can live their Catholic faith in peace and without unnecessary tension. To find that kind of culture is to find what Paul VI called the civilization of love or what Pope John Paul II spoke of when he called for a new Christian humanism. The popes are not calling for a Catholic "state" but for the creation of a culture that will be rich enough to provide means for expressing the Catholic faith in culturally distinctive fashion, a culture that will be resourceful enough to support the relationships of universal and local Catholic ecclesial communion.

An evangelized culture will offer no special favors to the Catholic Church. Creating a culture that provides a more evangelically authentic environment for daily life in the United States is less a program with clearly defined stages than a movement of gradual growth. Cultural change is slow, but it can be steady if our purpose is clear and our nerves are strong. We can pray also for moments of conversion, something like the revivalist movements that have marked our culture in the last century or in the nineteenth century. Nineteenth-century American converts to Catholicism such as Isaac Hecker, the founder of the Paulist Fathers, and Orestes Brownson, a great philosopher and social commentator of his day, were friends, engaged in conversation about why America must become Catholic. Their conversations bring us to particular moments when a culture can change. These are moments analogous to when a person changes.

Briefly, there are two kinds of change. First, there is the kind of change that is about fulfillment. A moment of fulfillment arises when we recognize that while life is fairly good, it is not complete; thus, we look for something more. That moment can occur in American culture itself when we recognize the good things in American society while, nonetheless, also recognizing that there is always more and so turn for fulfillment and perfection in the Catholic faith. Alternatively, there is the kind of change encountered in moments of healing. for instance, when there is a breakdown of some sort, such as when an individual faces the loss of a job, the diagnosis of terminal cancer, or the break-up of a marriage or family. Such persons know that they need to be healed and therefore need to be redeemed and saved by something outside of themselves. Analogously, whole cultures can also come to that moment when things are not going well at all and when they understand their need for a savior, a healer, someone to "put things back together" in the midst of a great national tragedy. We cannot pray for either of those two things as such, but we can pray for the conversion of our culture as well as of ourselves, our friends, and our families. In that prayer, evangelizers will come to a broad vision and will obtain strength for the long haul. Evangelizing culture relies on deep insight into the mysteries of our faith and keen vision for understanding the basis of our culture. To evangelize, it is not enough then to know the faith and to memorize the *Catechism* or Sacred Scripture. It is also important to understand the values, the history, the meanings, and the hierarchy of their importance in our culture.

Evangelizing culture is finally, then, a contemplative activity. The dialogue between Catholic faith and American culture takes place in the media, in the schools, in the marketplace, in the courts, and in the public square. But it begins truly in the heart of every American Catholic who loves both the Catholic faith and the American culture.

NOTES

1. For a more developed understanding of Cardinal George's views on the relation of faith and culture, see his following articles: "Catholic Faith and the Secular Academy," *Logos* 4:4 (Fall 2001): 73–81; "One Lord and One Church for One World," *Origins* 30:34 (February 8, 2001): 541, 543–49; "The Promotion of Missiological Studies in Seminaries," online at http://www.sedos.org/english/george_e.htm; "Law and Culture," *Ave Maria Law Review* 1:1 (Spring 2003): 1–17; "A New Apologetics for a New Evangelization," *Theology Digest* 47:4 (Winter 2000): 341–59; and "Public Morality in a Global Society: Catholics and Muslims in Dialogue," *Theology Digest* 49:4 (Winter 2002): 319–33.

2. Pope Paul VI, *Evangelii Nuntiandi* (Evangelization in the Modern World), December 8, 1975, no. 20.

3. The following analysis was developed in Francis E. George, "Evangelizing American Culture," *The New Catholic Evangelization*, ed. Kenneth Boyock, CSP (Mahwah, NJ: Paulist Press, 1992), 42–55.

4. John Paul II, Letter Instituting the Pontifical Council for Culture, May 20, 1982, *AAS*, LXXIV (1982), 683–88, as cited in *Towards a Pastoral Approach to Culture*, Pontifical Council for Culture, May 23, 1999, no. 1.

5. *Catechism of the Catholic Church*, no. 2333.

6

The Spirit of the Lord Is Upon Me

The Role of the Holy Spirit in the Work of Evangelization

Francis Martin

INTRODUCTION

St. Luke presented the opening event of Our Lord's public life as taking place in Nazareth (Luke 4:16–30). As a respected member of his former synagogue, Jesus was invited to read a passage from Isaiah, whether assigned to or chosen by him we do not know, and for Luke's purposes it made little difference. As he recorded this text—a combination of two Isaian passages—Luke intended to put the whole of Jesus's ministry under the theme of the Servant whose presence is evident throughout the Book of Isaiah. The beginning and continuance of the Servant's vocation derive from his anointing: the Spirit of the Lord rests upon him.

"The Spirit of the Lord is upon me,
for he has anointed me;
he has sent me to preach the Good News to the poor,
to proclaim release for prisoners
and sight for the blind,
to send the downtrodden away relieved,
and to proclaim the Lord's year of favor." (Luke 4:18–19)[1]

According to this passage, and indeed the whole of the New Testament, all genuine preaching of the good news, including that of Jesus himself, must take place under the anointing power of the Holy Spirit. In order to reinforce this truth, Luke quoted the risen Jesus as summing up the good news for his disciples, commanding them to preach it, and then, using the terms *power* and *promise* to refer to the Holy Spirit, sending them out to witness:

> Then he opened their minds to understand the scriptures, and he said to them, "Thus it is written, that the Messiah is to suffer and to rise from the dead on the third day, and that repentance and forgiveness of sins is to be proclaimed in his name to all nations, beginning from Jerusalem. You are witnesses of these things. And see, I am sending upon you what my Father promised; so stay here in the city until you are clothed with power from on high. (Luke 24:45–49)

This same injunction is repeated in the opening lines of the Book of Acts, which thus places the whole of the Church's life under the same power of the Holy Spirit that Jesus received at his baptism and poured out at pentecost (see Acts 2:33).

> While staying with them, he ordered them not to leave Jerusalem, but to wait there for the promise of the Father. "This," he said, "is what you have heard from me; for John baptized with water, but you will be baptized with the Holy Spirit not many days from now....You will receive power when the Holy Spirit has come upon you; and you will be my witnesses in Jerusalem, in all Judea and Samaria, and to the ends of the earth." (Acts 1:4–5, 8)

In all the texts just cited we can see a rhythm to the work of the Holy Spirit in the Church: the believers must first be acted upon by the Holy Spirit before they are able to bear witness and preach. They must, to use Luke's terminology here, wait to be clothed with power, wait for the promise of the Father; they must be baptized with the Holy Spirit. Then they will be witnesses to the end of the earth.

I wish in this chapter to reflect on this rhythm as we seek to look honestly at the obstacles to evangelization in our time, to learn solutions from the Lord, and, in the power of the Holy Spirit, to bring people into union with him. I will base this reflection on the Johannine writings. First, I will consider how the Church, individually and corporately, receives the action of the Holy Spirit in order to evangelize. Then, in some concluding reflections, I will reflect on what it means to make Christ manifest in our world and bring people to a genuine hope.

Part One
THE SPIRIT OF THE LORD IS UPON ME

The baptism of infants concludes with a ceremony that alludes to the healing that Jesus performed for a deaf man whose speech was impeded (Mark 7:31–37). Jesus put his fingers into the deaf man's ears, touched his tongue with his own spittle, groaned, and commanded: *Ephphatha!* The man could then hear and speak clearly.[2] The baptizing minister touches the infant's ears and mouth saying: "The Lord Jesus made the deaf hear and the dumb speak. May he soon touch your ears to receive his word, and your mouth to proclaim his faith, to the praise and glory of God the Father."

The Giver of Life

There is one text in the Johannine writings that briefly describes the role of the Spirit in bringing the work of Christ to life within the spirit of the believer. Within the concluding major section of 1 John 5:1–12, which is dedicated to the theme "faith as the principle of life,"[3] is this:

> He is the one who came through water and blood, Jesus Christ. Not in water only, but in water and in blood; and the Spirit is the one bearing witness, because the Spirit is the truth. Yes, there are three bearing witness: the Spirit and the water and the blood and the three are of one accord. (1 John 5:6–8)

I wish to call attention first of all to the tenses of the verbs used to describe the activity of Jesus Christ and the Spirit respectively. Jesus Christ "came"—literally, he is the "caming one," an impossible expression in English since we have nothing corresponding to the aorist participle (*o elthōn*), while the Spirit is the One "bearing witness" *now in the present* (*to marytoun*); what Jesus has accomplished still exists in his glorified humanity; it becomes alive and life-giving in history by the action of the Holy Spirit.

The activity of Jesus is described as coming "through water and blood." This refers to his baptism and passion. In the first of these events, Jesus irrevocably committed himself to his vocation as the Servant of God. He went to his cousin John and was baptized by him both as a sign of solidarity with a people who stood in need of repentance and as an expression of acceptance of his unique realization of his Israelite vocation. This is surely the way in which the gospel tradition gives us an interpretive narration of Jesus's baptism.[4] The enigmatic phrase in Matthew 3:15 concerning the fulfillment of all justice is best explained as the accomplishment of the Father's plan.[5]

The revelation Jesus received at his baptism confirmed and opened up for him this vocation as Servant of God. By using the opening words of the first servant song, Luke shows us that it was not for *his* sins that Jesus was baptized but for those of the whole people, indeed, those of the whole world.

> This means that Jesus is baptized in view of his death which effects forgiveness of sins for all men. For this reason Jesus must unite himself in solidarity with his whole people, and go down himself to Jordan, that 'all righteousness might be fulfilled.'...Jesus' reply [to the Baptist], which exegetes have always found difficult to explain, acquires a concrete meaning: Jesus will effect a general forgiveness....
>
> Thus the Baptism of Jesus points forward to the end, to the climax of his life, the Cross, in which alone all Baptism will find its fulfillment. There Jesus will achieve a general Baptism. In his own Baptism in the Jordan he received commission to do this.[6]

The insistence here that Jesus's coming was "not in water only" reflects the understanding of the early Church that by his baptism Jesus was oriented to his death for all. Jesus came also "in blood," that is, his passion. It is quite likely that the linking of water and blood in this text is meant to refute the initial stages of a heresy later identified with a certain Cerinthus, who claimed that Jesus received an empowerment at his baptism so that his teaching was of a particular force and wisdom but that this power left him at his crucifixion.[7] Such an approach to Jesus, a selective admiration of his teaching and an avoidance of his death and resurrection, has characterized Gnostic teaching up to our own day, as can be seen in the Jesus Seminar.

The understanding of Jesus's baptism as pointing toward and including his death and resurrection is witnessed to by Jesus's own use of baptismal vocabulary when referring to his vocation.[8] It is the witness of the Spirit that provided the inner and living understanding of this connection between baptism and death in Jesus and in us. The past actions of Jesus are still life-giving today because they are still present to us by the action of the Holy Spirit. Indeed, without this action the words of the sacred text and the liturgical gestures that reenact Jesus's gestures are unable to give rise to a life-giving experience.

A difficult and, at the same time, a most important aspect of the Johannine text we are considering (1 John 5:1–12) consists in the words that follow the statement that the Spirit is the Witnessing One, that is, the One who makes the words and actions of Jesus actually present in the community and in the life of the individual believer (v. 6). The text goes on to say that all of this takes place "because the Spirit is the truth."[9] Ignace de la Potterie correctly identifies this phrase as similar to several such phrases in the Johannine literature: "God is spirit" (John 4:24), for instance, is not a statement about the incorporeal nature of God but a declaration that God makes himself known and shares himself with us in and through the Holy Spirit. Similarly, "God is light" (1 John 1:5) and "God is love" (1 John 4:8, 16) refer to God as God manifests himself to us and acts in our regard ("light"), to the fact that God gives himself to us, and perhaps as well to the manner in which God the Father gives himself ineffably to the Son ("love"). These statements differ from Jesus's self-identification in the phrase "I am (*egō eimi*) the Way and the Truth and the Life," where he is describing himself as the Way to the Father precisely because he is in his very being not the revealer of the Father but the *Revelation* of the Father and the Life of those who accept that revelation. As Aquinas expresses it in the prologue to the third part of the *Summa Theologiae:* "Our Savior, the Lord Jesus Christ,...showed us the *way* of *truth* in himself through which we are able, rising, to arrive at the blessedness of immortal *life*...."

The witnessing action of the Spirit consists in that activity by which he brings us into living contact with Jesus, who, forever fixed in the act of love in which he died, is the abiding Revelation of the Father, and as such is the Truth. This action of the Holy Spirit takes place in the Church through the liturgy and the sacraments, by his direct action in the souls of the believers, and, as we will see, by the "works" of the disciples in their own witness to the truth. In regard to the first mode of witnessing, we have many descriptions in the fathers of the church. Let this statement of St. Leo represent their position: All those things which the Son of God both did and taught for the reconciliation of the world, we not only know in the account of things now past, but we also experience in the power of works which are present.[10]

That Leo intended by this to refer not only to the sacraments of the Church but also to the reading of the scriptures is evident from his oft-repeated notion that the gospel text, when received by faith, *makes present* that which it speaks about. Thus, he says that in the liturgical observance of the feast of the Epiphany,[11] "when the Gospel narrative/event *(evangelica historia)* is ceaselessly repeated, this mystery of salvation, brought about by a striking miracle, is always more profoundly imprinted on the minds of those who understand it."[12]

He Does Not Give the Spirit in Measure

In order to understand the second mode of the Spirit's witnessing, already implied in the above description of the reality mediated by scripture "imprinted on the mind," I will consider another Johannine text, chosen from many that would be apt, to show again the relation between the word of Jesus and the Spirit. By *word*, here I mean his being as expressed in his words and actions:

"Do you not believe that I am in the Father and the Father in me? The words that I say to you I do not speak on my own authority, but the Father who dwells in me does his works. Believe me that I am in the Father and the Father in me; or else believe me for the sake of the works themselves." (John 14:10–11)

The passage in John 3:31–36 is best understood as a Johannine commentary on the preceding section, which records the Baptist's witness to Jesus as the Bridegroom and himself as his friend. The evangelist goes on to declare that "the one coming from above is above all," and because he is from heaven, he speaks of what he has seen and heard though no one accepts his testimony. However, "He who receives his testimony sets his seal to this that God is true." We then find this statement: "For he whom God has sent utters the words of God, for it is not by measure that he gives the Spirit." Some interpret this to mean that this Envoy of the Father declares the words of God in a special way because "he," that is, the *Father*, has given the Spirit to Jesus "without measure," thus contrasting Jesus with a late attested rabbinic description of the prophets who received the Spirit "by weight" (*bmšql*).[13] It is more likely that John is saying that Jesus, the One sent from God, declares (*lalei*) the words of God in a unique way because he, *Jesus*, gives the Spirit without measure (*ouk ek metrou*). He is the One who baptizes in the Spirit (John 1:34), the One from whose "midst" flow rivers of living water, that is, the water of the Spirit that flowed along with the life-giving blood from the side of Jesus at the cross (John 7:37–39, 19:34).[14] In either interpretation the basic position is clear: It is because the words that Jesus speaks are delivered along with the gift of the Spirit without measure that they are in a unique and proper way "the words of God." The role of the Spirit is to stir up faith so that which is said is received for what it is.

In this text the fundamental structure of revelation according to St. John appears clearly: revelation is constituted formally by the words of Jesus, but these do not actually appear as the words *of God* except through the gift of the Spirit. Faith in the word is the fruit of the Spirit.[15]

When we consider the first quality of an evangelist, then, we must look for a Spirit-conferred experience of the *truth* of the Gospel.

Have I, or has anyone else aspiring to be an evangelist, received the grace of a personal encounter with the living Christ and come, at least initially, to know him *actually* as the Truth, the subsistent Revelation of the Father? Without this anointing, the written letter of the gospel itself can be death-dealing, as our tradition has always maintained:

> The Apostle says (2 Cor 3:6), "The letter brings death, but the Spirit gives life," and Augustine explains this (*De Spiritu et Litera* xiv, xvii) by saying that the letter denotes any writing external to man, even that of the moral precepts such as are contained in the Gospel. Wherefore the letter, even of the Gospel would kill, unless there were the inward presence of the healing grace of faith.[16]

Witness

Paul VI once stated: "Modern man listens more willingly to witnesses than to teachers, and if he does listen to teachers, it is because they are witnesses."[17] The importance of witness lies in this: that someone testifies to a contingent reality. Christian witness is a self-involving activity and it confers knowledge of something that cannot be deduced from general principles: it is known on the word of another because what is witnessed to is an event. It is obvious, then, that the Christian reality ultimately must be known personally and is received through the witness of another. Pope Benedict XVI began his first encyclical with these words: "Being Christian is not the result of an ethical choice or a lofty idea, but the encounter with an event, a person, which gives life a new horizon and a decisive direction."[18]

Testimony has two dimensions: it presents a contingent reality for interpretation and it involves the witness personally in the act of testifying. Proclaiming that Christ is risen from the dead is an activity different from maintaining that water begins to expand at 4° Centigrade.[19] The latter is stated and verified on the basis of empirical evidence; the former is verified only by yielding to the reality witnessed to under the action of the Holy Spirit: experience of the reality mediates the experienced reality to the recipient. This demands, first of all, that the witness be sent by God, who accomplishes this by accrediting the witness through an experience of the reality and by the steadfastness with which the witness proclaims the divinely wrought event even at the risk of security and life itself. Because the witness is sent, his testimony is corroborated by God himself: "We are witnesses to these things, as so is the Holy Spirit whom God has given to those who obey him" (Acts 5:32).

The Johannine Teaching on Witness

It should come as little surprise, then, to discover that in the Johannine literature that activity by which the Christian makes known what God has accomplished in Christ is described with the verb *martyrein*, "to witness, to bear personal testimony." It *may* come as a surprise to realize that the verb *to evangelize* (*euangelizesthai*) never occurs in this literature.[20] An evangelizer is a committed witness to what he or she knows personally, or he is no evangelizer at all.

This aspect of Johannine theology is part of a consistent view of the Christian's theater of action: it is the world. When this is sufficiently understood, we are able to appreciate the insistence in this inspired literature on the ambiguity of what is called *o kosmos*: "For God so loved the world that he gave his only Son, so that everyone who believes in him may not perish but may have eternal life" (John 3:16); "Do not love the world or the things in the world. The love of the Father is not in those who love the world" (1 John 2:15).

> The dualistic context is not for John a cosmic or metaphysical context. It is a spiritual structure which sets forth a reality of the moral order and which demonstrates at what depth salvation intervenes, what struggles it must face, what an abyss of pride and rebellion it must overcome. Johannine dualism is inscribed within a world of liberty and choice. The notion of "world" serves to unmask the demonic universe of refusal and rejection.[21]

John, the mystic, discerns behind the human forces that reject the message of salvation a "demonic universe of refusal and rejection" that put Christ on trial and killed him: "The devil had already put it into the heart of Judas son of Simon Iscariot to betray him" (John 13:2).[22] This vision explains the constant use of the verb *to witness* in the Johannine literature and the forensic overtones that it carries. As chapter 9 of the Gospel teaches us, the Christian is a healed blind beggar on trial: "Then I went and washed and received my sight" (John 9:11).[23] The Christian is a witness, driven by his or her own experience of the saving act of God and the conviction that this act is meant to give life to the whole world: "He is the atoning sacrifice for our sins, and not for ours only but also for the sins of the whole world" (1 John 2:2).

In the Johannine view, testimony follows upon direct knowledge: "Very truly, I tell you, we speak of what we know and testify to what we have seen; yet you people do not receive our testimony" (John 3:11). Jesus does speak of witnesses to himself (see John 5:31–32, 36, 37, 39; 8:14, 18, etc.). Most of the testimony, however, is given by others: John the Baptist (John 1:7–8, 25) and especially the disciples. The testimony is most often in regard to some historical event, but the object of the testimony has to do with its meaning. Thus, the opening lines of 1 John speak of a physical contact, yet the witness is of a spiritual reality: "What was from the beginning, what we have heard, what we have seen with our eyes, what we have looked at and touched with our hands, *concerning the word of life....*" We encounter the same rhythm, for instance, in regard to the blood and water from Christ's side (John 19:35), though in this passage the full reality of what is witnessed to must be gathered together from the promise of the water to come from the midst of Christ in John 7:38–39. Regarding the "works" of Christ, these are called a witness in John 5:36: "But I have a testimony greater than John's. The works that the Father has given me to complete, the very works that I am doing, testify on my behalf that the Father has sent me." Lucien Cerfaux says of all the "works" of Christ as John understands them: "The miracles of the Son, his 'works,' are in reality the work of the Father, his essential activity of creation and giving life; as we look upon these, we see in one and the same regard the Son and the Father whom he makes known."[24] The witness of the disciples, therefore, reaches its goal in the testimony to the true reality of Jesus.

The synthesis of all this testifying activity is found in John 15:26–27: "When the Paraclete comes, whom I shall send to you from the Father, the Spirit of truth who issues from the Father, he will be my witness. And you too will be witnesses, because you have been with me from the beginning." Outside the New Testament, the Greek term *paraclete* evokes a forensic environment: that of someone called in as a helper, counselor, advocate, and encourager in a legal proceeding—and only John uses the term in the New Testament. The Holy Spirit is called "another Paraclete" in the first of the five Paraclete promises (John 14:15–17, 25–26; 15:26–27; 16:7–11, 12–15) since the Johannine tradition considers Jesus as "the Paraclete" (1 John 2:1).

In the text that I have described as a synthesis of the witnessing activity of the disciples, the Paraclete is also called the "Spirit of truth," thus evoking a theme we have seen earlier. It is important to note that this passage is found in the middle of a long section (John 15:18—16:4) often entitled "The World's Hatred." Obviously, then, what is said here about witnessing is being presented in a context of a conflict sustained by the "demonic universe of refusal and rejection." The striking resemblance of this section to Synoptic passages has often been remarked upon.[25] Although the theme of divine aid in persecution is present in the Synoptic texts, there is never direct mention of the *witness* of the Spirit, which for John is an intrinsic part of the disciples' share in the Messianic persecutions.[26]

Let us look more closely now at the text of John 15:26–27:

> "When the Paraclete comes, whom I will send to you from
> the Father, the Spirit of Truth who will come forth from the
> Father, he will witness concerning me. Moreover, you will
> witness because you are with me from the beginning."

The words that follow immediately upon this passage are significant: "I have told you these things so that you be not scandalized" (John 16:1). In this situation, when the disciples are "on trial" before the tribune of the world and are enduring persecution, either mental or physical or both, the Paraclete, the Spirit of Truth, will witness to them concerning Jesus and will preserve them from falling away, even while they are bearing their own witness. What sustains the disciples of any age, including our own, is the living experience of the reality and majesty of Jesus Christ, who is with the Father.

In a moment we will consider the obstacles to our own witness, but it is important even here to follow the reasoning of the Fourth

Gospel. We must be realistic: Behind the cultural deficiencies and the mental and moral blindness that we may encounter as we witness to Jesus to our families, to our friends and acquaintances, and to groups of people we may be called upon to address, there is another force. When people accept the witness of the Spirit, we rejoice as they experience the truth of Jesus's promise that he will draw all people to himself and offer them salvation. At the same time, we must be aware of what this effort may cost us in terms of disappointment, fatigue, and misunderstanding, especially within the ranks of the Church itself, and even downright opposition. Jesus's promise of the other Paraclete will become an experiential reality at these moments. The Spirit of Truth sent by Jesus, the Divine Son, will come forth from the Father and give us assurance that the One to whom we bear witness is indeed with the Father and with us. In this sense the witness of the Spirit here is first and foremost an interior activity within the believer: "He will bear witness concerning me shining in your hearts and conferring a more perfect assurance."[27]

There is as well an exterior dimension to the witness of the Spirit that he works through the disciples. Jesus promises that the conviction and power of the interior witness of the Spirit will overflow in and through us as well as *we* witness. Paul gives a striking description of this reality in 1 Thessalonians 1:4–5: "For we know, brothers and sisters beloved by God, that he has chosen you, because our message of the gospel came to you not in words only, but also in power and in the Holy Spirit and with full conviction." It is most likely that the term *power* in the text refers to extraordinary manifestations of the Holy Spirit: miracles, healings, exorcisms, and so forth, as Paul also says: "The signs of a true apostle were performed among you with utmost patience, signs and wonders, and mighty works" (2 Cor 12:12). There are many accounts of such activity and the ensuing conversions narrated in the Acts of the Apostles. In the Thessalonians text already cited, Paul goes on to describe this process of conversion: "...how you turned to God from idols, to serve a living and true God, and to wait for his Son from heaven, whom he raised from the dead—Jesus, who rescues us from the wrath that is coming" (1 Thess 1:9–10).

In the light of the constant New Testament attestation of "signs and wonders and deeds of power," it is to be expected that the interior *martyrion* of the Holy Spirit to the disciple would be the foundation of a witness through the disciple to the world at large, and that this would include the same type of activity. We find a description of such activity in Jesus's promise: "Very truly, I tell you, the one who believes in me will also do the works that I do and, in fact, will do greater works than these, because I am going to the Father" (John 14:12). There are at least thirteen places where the term *works (erga)* refers to extraordinary manifestations of divine power.[28] Jesus says in John 14:10 that "the Father who dwells in me does his works," and similar statements are found elsewhere (John 5:36; 9:3–4; 10:25, 32, 37). It is through the "works" that one can be brought to faith that "I am in the Father and the Father is in me" (John 14:11).

The works of the disciples are, like the works of Jesus, "signs" manifesting the action of Jesus through the Holy Spirit in and through the one believing in him, and thus manifesting the Father. They are "greater" than Jesus's works not because they are more spectacular but because as "signs" they manifest the completed plan of God: Jesus Christ, the Incarnate Word of God in glory, acting in and through his disciples by the Holy Spirit, and thus, as the Truth, as the Revelation of the Father, making known his name. We have here another expression of the witness of the Spirit who is "the Truth" (1 John 5:6). In addition to the whole life of the Church, its scriptures, and its sacraments, and in addition to the interior witness within the disciples, the "works" of the disciples are a third mode of the Spirit's witnessing "concerning Jesus" and making him known. The works of the disciples ultimately reveal the Father: "Very truly, I tell you, whoever receives the one whom I send receives me; and whoever receives me receives him who sent me" (John 13:20).

Overcoming the Obstacles

In this last section of this part of my study, I wish to remain at the Johannine level of analysis for one more step: namely, John's understanding of the profound reasons why the world is sinfully wrong and why it is important that the believer understand this in order to have courage and understanding in the task of evangelization. The reflection will be based on the fourth of the Paraclete promises in John 16:7–11. The text is as follows:

"Nevertheless I tell you the truth: it is to your advantage that I go away, for if I do not go away, the Advocate will not come to you; but if I go, I will send him to you. And when he comes, he will prove the world wrong about sin and righteousness and judgment: about sin, because they do not believe in me; about righteousness, because I am going to the Father and you will see me no longer; about judgment, because the ruler of this world has been condemned."

The essential action of the Paraclete in this passage is to prove that the world is culpably wrong, to establish its culpability as *world*. The difficulty arises when we seek to define the recipient of this action. Is it that the world is brought to acknowledge its sin or that the believers are given irrefutable proof that the world is in sin? Basically, it must be the second. If the world were able to acknowledge its sin, it would no longer be the "world," that is, a place which, despite the fact that there is still room for freedom and choice, is nevertheless at its depths a "demonic universe of refusal and rejection." The "world" would become "kingdom." The Greek verb used here (*elenchein*) evokes the notion of establishing or revealing a fault, often in an unmistakably forensic context.[29] Of the several possible nuances available, only one seems adequate to describe the Spirit's action here: he will afford convincing proof that the world is wrong and in sin.

Once this is established in the heart of the believer, we may allow for the rhythm encountered in the previous Paraclete passage: The Spirit's primary action takes place within the spirit of the believer, proving the world wrong. This, however, can then enable the believers, now free from the illusions offered by the world, to offer to those in the world who will accept their testimony (the Spirit's testimony) a way to Life. In practice, however, the rhythm is not that clear cut. Though the believer has passed from death to life and has the witness of the Spirit within him, there are still areas of darkness that need to be yielded to the action of the same Spirit. In fact, it is in experiencing these in himself that the believer can understand the terrifying dynamics of the struggle between light and darkness and be a credible witness to the lies of the world and the joy of overcoming these and believing the Truth: "And his commandments are not burdensome, for whoever is born of God conquers the world. And this is the victory that conquers the world, our faith" (1 John 5:3–4).

The remarks of Jesus here are in response to the fact that, when Jesus spoke of his departure, grief filled the hearts of the disciples (John 16:6). But the fact of the matter is that, when Jesus "goes" and is glorified, the disciples will be able to know him in a new way and thus also see the Father in a new way (John 14:9). They should not be grieved or distressed, they are not orphans, and the Spirit will enable them to overcome the obstacles presented by the world. The obstacles, then, are a culpably distorted view of three realities: sin, justice, and judgment. We can touch on each of these only briefly.

"IN REGARD TO SIN, BECAUSE THEY DO NOT BELIEVE IN ME"

The root sin of the world is refusal to believe in Jesus and the place he holds next to the Father as the Revelation of the Father; the root sin is to reject the Truth: "Whoever believes in the Son has eternal life; whoever disobeys the Son will not see life, but must endure God's wrath" (John 3:36). Also:

> "The one who rejects me and does not receive my word has a judge; on the last day the word that I have spoken will serve as judge, for I have not spoken on my own, but the Father who sent me has himself given me a commandment about what to say and what to speak. And I know that his commandment is eternal life. What I speak, therefore, I speak just as the Father told me." (John 12:48–50)

These texts, and others that could be adduced, are speaking of the objective sin of the rejection of the Father's revelation in Jesus. Such rejection is implied in *every* sin and can ultimately lead to outright and explicit rejection.

For example, some people who consistently and vigorously promote abortion run this risk. Implied in the whole issue of abortion is the simple question: Is there a God and does he have the right to tell us what to do? Someone who has personally resolved this question through the action of the Holy Spirit, and who has thus suffered through to fidelity in other areas of life, sees in the light of the Holy Spirit how what he or she has experienced is a paradigm of what the sin of the world really is. Such a person can then address people with conviction and compassion.

"IN REGARD TO JUSTICE, BECAUSE I GO TO THE FATHER AND YOU NO LONGER SEE ME"

The word translated as "justice" (*dikaiosunē*) can have the usual English meaning of "justice," "uprightness," and so forth, but in the Bible, under the influence of the Hebrew word *ṣedeq*, it can mean "vindication" or "victory," as in the short hymn recorded in 1 Timothy 3:16: "Without any doubt, the mystery of our religion is great: He was revealed in flesh, vindicated [from the root *dikaioun*] in spirit, seen by angels, proclaimed among Gentiles, believed in throughout the world, taken up in glory."[30]

The world is culpably in error because it refuses to accept the resurrection of Jesus with all that this implies regarding the identity of God, the dignity of a human existence, the fruit of obedience to God, and goal of human history. The result of this aberration is that life becomes meaningless and we strive to fill the void by following the deception of disordered desire. At this level of human existence, the obstacles to evangelization are evident. They are evident not only in individual lives but in the hopelessness and the depression that result from the trivialization of human existence characteristic of much of Western life in its cultural expression.

Evangelization may often mean offering the light of the resurrection as it is refracted through friendship, love, and community. Thus the Risen Christ meets the person and can make himself known as the Truth, the Revelation of the Father, long before this becomes explicit in a person's perception. Ultimately, Jesus, as risen from the dead, "justifies" his own risk, which every believer must imitate, namely, that ultimately love and sacrifice are more powerful than violence and death. This is to undo the lie and the fear of death hidden in the world's refusal to hear the witness of the resurrection: "Since, therefore, the children share flesh and blood, he himself likewise shared the same things, so that through death he might destroy the one who has the power of death, that is, the devil, and free those who all their lives were held in slavery by the fear of death" (Heb 2:14–15).

"ABOUT CONDEMNATION, BECAUSE THE PRINCE OF THIS WORLD HAS BEEN CONDEMNED"

The worship of power is a form of idolatry and it is based on the illusion that power is a transcendent reality. The world esteems power as the highest good, and this is especially true of the culture in which we live. Those who would evangelize must neither be attached to power nor afraid of it. When the Church fails to see the lie in a false understanding of power, she falls victim to the three temptations that faced Jesus in the desert, so admirably described by Fyodor Dostoyevsky in the words of the Grand Inquisitor, who accuses Jesus of failing to use the power offered him in the illusion that human response to God must be free:

> We have corrected your great work and have based it on miracle, mystery, and authority. And men rejoiced that they were once more led like sheep and that the terrible gift which had brought them so much suffering had at last been lifted from their hearts. You could have taken over all the power, the authority of this world when that spirit showed you the kingdoms and rulers of the world. But you rebuked him, and that power crucified you. *Why did you reject that last gift? By accepting that third counsel of the mighty spirit, you would have accomplished all that man seeks on earth, that is to say, whom to worship (the source of miracle), to whom to entrust his conscience (the possessor of mystery) and how at last to unite all in a common, harmonious, and incontestable ant-hill, for the need of universal unity is the third and last torment of men.*[31]

The world's dream of untrammeled power, the ability to work one's will and overcome all obstacles, lies at the heart of all the totalitarian systems that were responsible for the deaths of uncountable millions in our own time: there are few who cannot see the lie of Satan, the enemy of humankind, as the primary actor in this tragedy. The allure of a future utopia as the triumph of human effort has always served as the justification of oppression and murder. It is a failure to see that the prince of this world has already been condemned. As Jesus faced his impending passion he solemnly declared its result: "Now is the judgment of this world; now the ruler of this world will be driven out" (John 12:31). The power of the prince of this world is illusory and not to be feared: "Little children, you are from God, and have conquered them [false prophets]; for the one who is in you is greater than the one who is in the world" (1 John 4:4).

The role of the Holy Spirit is to bring the spirit of the believer to penetrate the "pomp of power" and see behind it the ultimate powerlessness of the illusions embraced by the world. This can then allow the believer to witness to the truth that frees people from the judgment already laid on darkness.

I will conclude this part of my study with these dramatic words that once again show us where judgment really lies and what the goal of all evangelization is: to eliminate those forces that keep people back from coming to the light, and to help them attain freedom.

> [And Jesus said:] "Indeed, God did not send the Son into the world to condemn the world, but in order that the world might be saved through him. Those who believe in him are not condemned; but those who do not believe are condemned already, because they have not believed in the name of the only Son of God. And this is the judgment, that the light has come into the world, and people loved darkness rather than light because their deeds were evil. For all who do evil hate the light and do not come to the light, so that their deeds may not be exposed. But those who do what is true come to the light, so that it may be clearly seen that their deeds have been done in God." (John 3:17–21)

Part Two
CONCLUDING REFLECTIONS

All that I have tried to say here can be summed up aptly in Pope Benedict XVI's observation, during his first homily at the Basilica of St. John Lateran, that Christ is in need of witnesses who know him and have, as it were, actually touched him.[32] To have touched Christ in the force of the Holy Spirit is to have been changed by him in an intimate encounter. This is the foundation of all evangelization. Not only must we know what we are talking about, we must also share the compassion of Christ, which is the source of all gospel preaching:

> When he saw the crowds, he had compassion for them, because they were harassed and helpless, like sheep without a shepherd. Then he said to his disciples, "The harvest is plentiful, but the laborers are few; therefore ask the Lord of the harvest to send out laborers into his harvest." (Matt 9:36–38; see also Mark 6:34; Matt 14:14)

Culture and Evangelization: Brief Remarks

ANALYSIS

The challenge, briefly expressed by John Paul II, is to so live and experience the divine realities mediated to us by the Church that they achieve a cultural expression. A faith that does not become culture, he said, has never fully matured.[33] The first step in enabling a faith to become culture is to look at our own cultural environment in order to understand where it impedes and where it furthers the full expression of faith among ourselves. After all, our own minds are the first audience to which we must preach the gospel. The second step is to effect a correlation between our culture and the faith of the Church, allowing a faith-vision to engage the culture and take up into the gospel all that is true and positive in the culture, while correcting or even rejecting those aspects that can be seen to be false in the light of faith.[34]

John Paul II also named nonbelief, along with the secularization, religious indifference, and rejection of religion that follow in its wake, as a most urgent matter for reflection and pastoral concern. He urged that its historical, cultural, social, and intellectual causes be sought, and he expressed the conviction that open dialogue with nonbelievers and nonadherents to any religion would be productive.[35]

RESPONSE

The primary response to the problems of our world is a faith that is "fully received, thoroughly thought through, and fully lived out" and thus becomes an alternate culture.[36] Cultures require community on both a familial and a broader level. This points to the need for renewing parishes, and thus to the need for authentic liturgies where there is praise (with music that supports such praise), reverence (including manner of dress), genuine preaching so that, from these Eucharistic liturgies, "the source and summit of the Christian life,"[37] experiential faith may grow and be communicated in the activities of the parish, especially in catechetics, evangelization, and care for the poor.

A particularly important aspect of forging an alternate culture is found in that work of the Holy Spirit raising up new communities and movements that are not meant to be competitors but, rather, collaborators with the parishes. In his discourse to the World Congress of the Ecclesial Movements held in Rome in 1998, Pope John Paul II stated that the institutional and charismatic aspects of the Church are both essential to its constitution. He emphasized the need for living Christian communities and identified his audience as among those capable of originating and sustaining such communities. True charisms, he added, always aim at the encounter with Christ in the sacraments.[38]

In these remarks, John Paul II indicates the direction for the new evangelization. As we have seen, the Holy Spirit's witness to our own human spirits can be direct. Believers are touched and come to a new and more personal experience of the risen Jesus Christ: this is the foundation for a mature faith. In the light of that faith, believers understand the situation of their environment and their culture, and they can see the spiritual light and darkness that lies behind our developing history. They are able then to address the people of their age: their friends, their neighbors, all their contemporaries. As St. John said of his own preaching: "We declare to you what we have seen and heard so that you also may have fellowship with us; and truly our fellowship is with the Father and with his Son Jesus Christ. We are writing these things so that our joy may be complete" (1 John 1:3–4).

NOTES

1. Translation is from Joseph Fitzmyer, *The Gospel According to Luke (I–IX),* ed. William Foxwell Albright and David Noel Freedman, Anchor Bible 28 (New York: Doubleday, 1981), 525.

2. The theme of having the ears opened and then speaking/acting is found in the Old Testament: for example, see Isa 50:4–5; Ps 40:7 (MT).

3. Thus, we find in this section 5:1: "Everyone who believes that Jesus is the Christ has been born of God"; 5:11–12: "And this is the testimony: God gave us eternal life, and this life is in his Son. Whoever has the Son has life; whoever does not have the Son of God does not have life"; and 5:13, which is the conclusion of the section and of the letter: "I write these things to you who believe in the name of the Son of God, so that you may know that you have eternal life."

4. I refer the reader to the studies of Kilian McDonnell, *The Baptism of Jesus in the Jordan: The Trinitarian and Cosmic Order of Salvation* (Collegeville, MN: Liturgical Press, 1996) and of Joan Taylor, *The Immerser: John the Baptist within Second Temple Judaism* (Grand Rapids: Eerdmans, 1997).

5. "We are inclined to define the 'righteousness' of 3.15 as moral conduct: Jesus, knowing the messianic prophecies of the OT, obediently fulfills them and thereby fulfills all righteousness." W. D. Davies and Dale C. Allison, *The Gospel According to Saint Matthew: International Critical Commentary* (Edinburgh: T. & T. Clark, 1988), 1:326–27.

6. Oscar Cullman, *Baptism in the New Testament,* trans. J. K. S. Reid, *Studies in Biblical Theology* 1, ed. C. F. D. Moule and H. H. Rowley (London: SCM Press, 1950), 18–19.

7. For a brief discussion, see Rudolf Schnackenburg, *The Johannine Epistles: A Commentary,* trans. Reginald and Ilse Fuller (New York: Crossroad, 1992), 233.

8. "I have a baptism with which to be baptized, and what stress I am under until it is completed!" (Luke 12:50); "But Jesus said to them, 'You do not know what you are asking. Are you able to drink the cup that I drink, or to be baptized with the baptism that I am baptized with?'" (Mark 10:38).

9. For what follows I am indebted to the study by Ignace de la Potterie, *La Vérité dans Saint Jean, Analecta Biblica*, 73/74 (Rome: Pontifical Biblical Institute, 1977), 315–28.

10. *On the Passion* 12 (*Sources Chrétiennes* 74, 82).

11. Leo is speaking of the liturgical reading. See *Sacrosanctum Concilium* 7: "Christ is present in his word, in that he himself is speaking when Scripture is read in the Church."

12. *On the Epiphany* 5 (*Sources Chrétiennes* 22, 254). See also *On the Resurrection* 1 (*Sources Chrétiennes* 74, 123); *On the Passion* 5, 18 (*Sources Chrétiennes* 41, 74, 112). For the references to these citations, see Dom Marie-Bernard de Soos, "Le Mystère Liturgique d'après saint Léon le Grand" (doctoral thesis, Toulouse, June 10, 1955).

13. *Lev. Rab.* 15, 2. Commentators regularly cite H. L. Strack and P. Billerbeck, *Kommentar zum Neuen Testament aus Talmud und Midrasch* (Munich: C. H. Beck'sche Verlagsbuchhandlung, 1965), 2:431.

14. "The Envoy of God speaks the words of God because he gives the Spirit without measure." Translation of Origen, Fragment 48, 11. 5–7, in *Die Griechischen Christlichen Schriftstellar der Ersten Drei Jahrhunderte, Origenes IV* (Leipzig: J. C. Hinrichs'sche Buchhandlung, 1903), 523.

15. Ignace de la Potterie, "Parole et Esprit dans S. Jean," in *L'Évangile de Jean. Sources, Rédaction, Théologie*, ed. M. de Jong, *Bibliotheca Ephemeridum Theologicarum Lovaniensium* 44 (Gembloux: Duculot, 1977), 184.

16. Thomas Aquinas, *Summa Theologiae* I–II, 106, 2.

17. *Evangelii Nuntiandi* 41.

18. *Deus Caritas Est* 1.

19. The remarks to follow are indebted to the remarkable essay by Paul Ricoeur, "The Hermeneutics of Testimony," in *Essays on Biblical Interpretation*, ed. Lewis S. Mudge (Philadelphia: Fortress, 1980), 119–54.

20. The verb does come once in Rev 14:6: "Then I saw another angel flying in midheaven, with an eternal gospel [*euangelion*] to pro-

claim [*euangelisai*] to those who live on the earth—to every nation and tribe and language and people."

21. Donatien Mollat, *St. Jean. Maître Spirituel, Bibliothèque de Spiritualité* 10 (Paris: Beauchesne, 1976), 27.

22. One should also consult the references to the "ruler of this world" in John 11:31, 14:30.

23. See also Luke 21:13, Mark 13:9, Matt 10:18.

24. Lucien Cerfaux, "Les miracles, signes messianiques de Jésus et oeuvres de Dieu selon l'Évangile de saint Jean," in *Recueil Lucien Cerfaux*, 2:48, as cited by Ignace de la Potterie, "La Notion de témoignage dans saint Jean," in *Sacra Pagina* (Paris: Gembloux, 1959), 201, n 2.

25. I give here a partial list of parallel words and themes. "A" in the parentheses refers to the number in Kurt Aland, *Synopsis of the Four Gospels* (Stuttgart: United Bible Societies, 1972). HATED BY EVERYBODY: John 15:18–19, 22–25 (A.100: Matt 10:22), also (A.289: Matt 24.9–10ff); SERVANT NOT GREATER: John 15:20, also 13.16 (A.100: Matt 10:24; Luke 6:40); WILL PERSECUTE YOU: John 15:20c (A.100: Matt 10:23; Luke 21:12); BECAUSE OF MY NAME: John 15:21 (only here in John), Matt 10:22, 24:9ff; SPIRIT FROM THE FATHER: John 15:26 (A.100: Matt 10:20) (also A.289: Mark 13:19–27); SCANDAL: John 16:1 (A.289: Matt 24:10).

26. However, see Acts 5:32, 6:10.

27. Euthymius Zigabenus, commenting on this passage (*PG* 129, 1420A). Cited by de la Potterie, *Verité*, 395, n 189.

28. John 5:20, 36; 7:3; 9:3, 4; 10:25, 32, 37; 14:10, 11, 12; 15:24.

29. For a complete treatment of this word, one may consult de la Potterie, *Verité*, 399–406.

30. Significant for our purposes is a fifth-century Egyptian manuscript known as the Freer Logion, which contains another ending to the Gospel of Mark. Twice it refers to the victory/vindication of Jesus at his resurrection using the term *dikaiosunē*: "This age of lawlessness and unbelief is under Satan, who by means of evil spirits does not permit the true power of God to be apprehended: therefore reveal your righteousness [*dikaiosunē*] now....[Jesus replied,] 'The limit of the years of the authority of Satan has been fulfilled, but other terrible things draw near even for sinners on whose behalf I was delivered up to death, that they might turn to the truth and sin no more, in order that they may inherit the spiritual and incorruptible glory of righteousness [*dikaiosunē*] which is in heaven.'"

Translation by Vincent Taylor, *The Gospel According to St. Mark* (New York: MacMillan & Co Ltd, 1957), 614–15.

31. Fyodor Dostoyevsky, *The Brothers Karamazov*, trans. David Magarshack (Middlesex, England: Penguin Books, 1958), 301–2. The lines in italic are in the original.

32. Pope Benedict XVI, "Homily, Mass of Possession of the Chair: St. John Lateran Basilica," in *L'Osservatore Romano* (English edition) 19 (May 11, 2005), 3.

33. From the letter founding the Pontifical Council for Culture, March 3, 1982, in Michael Paul Gallagher, *Clashing Symbols: An Introduction to Faith and Culture* (London: Darton, Longman and Todd Ltd, 1997), 53.

34. Pope John Paul II, "Discourse to the Plenary Assembly of the Pontifical Council for Culture" 3, delivered on January 18, 1983. The English translation of this address can be found on the Vatican website: www.vatican.va. For the original text, see "La Chiesa creatrice di cultura nel suo rapporto con il mondo moderno," in *L'Osservatore Romano* (Italian edition) 123, no. 14 (January 19, 1983), 1.

35. Address of March 18, 1994.

36. This is a positive rephrasing of Pope John Paul II's statement: "The faith that has not become culture is *not* fully received, *not* entirely thought through, *not* faithfully lived." Italics added. The original comes from the pope's March 3, 1982, letter founding the Pontifical Council for Culture.

37. *Lumen Gentium* 11.

38. Pope John Paul II, "Address of His Holiness John Paul II on the Occasion of the Meeting with the Ecclesial Movements and the New Communities, Rome, 30 May 1998," in *Movements in the Church: Proceedings of the World Congress of the Ecclesial Movements, Rome, 27–29 May 1998, The Laity Today* (Vatican City: Pontificium Consilium pro Laicis, 1999), 221–23.

From Maintenance to Mission

Evangelization and the Revitalization of the Parish

Robert Rivers, CSP

Introduction

I must confess that I am part of the rare breed, diminished in number but not extinct, of golfing priests. Some years ago I gained great insight into my golf game while playing with one of my parishioners at the prestigious Bel Air Country Club in Los Angeles. I had enough opportunities to play there that my friend Ralph, who is Jerry Ormand's regular caddy, knew me and my game quite well. Ralph was a very wise, gentle, and experienced caddy who was always very positive with his patrons. He would never say, "Don't hit it in the lake," or "Don't slice it into the woods," or "Make sure you avoid the bunkers." Rather, he was always very encouraging: "Padrecito, hit it to me!" or "Put it right down the center!" I was what you might call a "Dickensian golfer": It was either the best of times or the worst of times for this golfing priest; it was never in between. This particular day it was the worst of times. For sixteen holes I slashed and chopped and scraped out a pretty disgraceful path on this beautiful course—at which point Ralph, lovingly and gently, came up to me and said, "Padrecito. You are a good priest." (The unspoken message was: "Don't quit your day job.")

Now I *do* have a reason for beginning with a golf story. I want to offer a golf metaphor for all of us who are trying to move our parishes from maintenance to mission. The metaphor is taken from Tiger Woods, arguably the best professional golfer of this era. It is based upon my conviction that Tiger Woods's incomparable record comes not because he is the best shot maker in the business but because he is a "grinder."

Now, what the sports analysts mean by a grinder is somebody who never gives up, who gives his or her all to every shot no matter what kind of a day they are having. I submit that in this business of evangelization we need to have the virtue of the grinder, rather than the spectacular flash of occasional brilliance. The reason Tiger Woods wins so many tournaments is that he never gives up, he hardly ever shoots himself out of a tournament, and he never depends on having "a good day" as the foundation for being a winner. Rather, he depends upon his virtue of hanging in there, giving it his best shot in whatever circumstances he finds himself, and persevering for the long run.

This quality of being a grinder has won him a lot of tournaments and is essential to understanding his phenomenal success. It is not a virtue that we associate with a great golfer of Woods's stature, nor, perhaps, is it a virtue that is high on *our* list, we who are the Lord's evangelizers. But it should be!

Becoming a grinder like Tiger Woods could take us very far in our efforts to move from maintenance to missionary parishes, which is the subject of my two-part essay. First, let's explore what it means and why we need to move our parishes from maintenance to mission. Second, let's consider how we can do this successfully.

From Maintenance to Mission
What Does It Mean?
Why Should We Make This Move?

When I use the expression to "move from maintenance to mission," I am simply putting into a practical phrase a profound theological truth that most people already know. Pope Paul VI and his successors have told us that evangelization is the essential mission of the Church and therefore the essential mission of every parish.

Evangelization is part and parcel of the renewal of the Second Vatican Council, which we have been implementing now for the past forty years. In fact, Cardinal Avery Dulles stated, in a talk that he gave on the twentieth anniversary of Paul VI's *On Evangelization in the Modern World,* that the pope gave us a new interpretation of the purpose of the Second Vatican Council—which was evangelization. The pope told us that the purpose of the council was better to prepare the *Church* of the twentieth century to proclaim the good news to the *world* in the twentieth century. In other words, the entire purpose of the council was to do interior renewal for the sake of exterior mission—not a bad definition of evangelization.

So the first point I want to make is that this movement from maintenance to mission at the parish level is simply another way of speaking about the Church's essential mission of evangelization and about mission being an integral part of the renewal of the Second Vatican Council. In fact, one could make the claim, and I do in the opening chapters of my book *From Maintenance to Mission: Evangelization and the Revitalization of the Parish,* that evangelization is the crown jewel of the renewal. It is the integrating perspective that enables us to better understand what we have been doing for these past forty years as we've implemented various aspects of the council's reform agenda.

Now for the even more critical follow-up point: Pope Paul VI, in *On Evangelization in the Modern World,* emphasized that "evangelizing all people constitutes the essential mission of the Church....It is the grace and favor proper to the Church, her deepest identity....[The Church] exists in order to evangelize" (14). We have no option but to become missionary parishes. It is not acceptable for us to assume a maintenance posture. Pope John Paul II also stated this very strongly when he said: "No Christian community is faithful to its duty unless it is missionary: either it is a Missionary Community or it is not even a Christian community, because these are simply two dimensions of the same reality, which is brought about by baptism and the other sacraments."[1]

Given the mandate that we all have, then, to create missionary-rather than maintenance-oriented parishes, what are we talking about? I can zero in on the essence of what I want to say by relating a conversation I had with some of my parishioners at St. Paul the Apostle in Los Angeles. One Sunday after Mass an elderly couple, Joseph and Mary, came up to me and said: "Now, Father, all this talk about evangelization is great. But who is going to take care of us while you're out there taking care of them?" The "them," presumably, are inactive Catholics and people with no church family. Note that behind Mary and Joseph's statement of concern contain several presumptions that we want to examine.

The first presumption is the inclusive/exclusive framework in which Mary and Joseph spoke. They distinguished between "us" and "them." "Us" referred to the faithful folks who come to Mass every Sunday, and "them" referred to all those people who, for various reasons, are not part of "us." As a matter of fact, my friends understood something intuitively that Paulist evangelizers Frs. Frank DeSiano and Kenneth Boyack point out very astutely in their book *Creating the Evangelizing Parish*: parishes typically organize themselves along these exclusion/inclusion lines.[2] The parish *seems* to exist for the sake of the membership. But this is a very questionable premise indeed.

The second presumption of Mary and Joseph's statement is that evangelization is a kind of quixotic, optional activity in which their pastor is choosing to engage. They are concerned that whatever evangelization is all about, the pastor needs to make sure that it doesn't interfere with his primary responsibility, which is to take care of the needs of the membership. Had Mary and Joseph been familiar with the "job description" of pastors given to us in canon 528 of the *Code of Canon Law*, they might have viewed the matter differently. It states that "the pastor is obliged to see to it that the word of God in its entirety is announced to those living in the parish...and he is to make every effort with the aid of the Christian faithful, to bring the Gospel message also to those who have ceased practicing their religion or who do not profess the true faith."[3]

The final presumption is that evangelization obviously has nothing to do with them. Mary and Joseph were the best of the old-school, pre–Vatican II Catholics who, as Fr. Patrick Brennan says, see baptism as entitlement.[4] Brennan calls them "consumer Catholics." They come to church to get what they need to get to heaven. There is no clear sense of baptism as a call to share in the mission and ministry of Jesus, which, of course, is one of the principal teachings of the Second Vatican Council.

A maintenance-oriented parish is one in which the parish is focused on its current members, who absorb most of its time, energy, and resources. There is a preoccupation with "us" and a general forgetting about "them." Or, to put it another way, our members, in their consumer consciousness, have very little sense of their own missionary calling. As a consequence, our parishes, by and large, are not mission-oriented but maintenance-oriented. Our time and energy as parishes are absorbed by taking care of ourselves.

The picture is clear. Now the questions we might raise are: What's wrong with that? Why should we change? I know some pastors who don't want to create missionary parishes that reach out to those who are absent, because those pastors feel they already have too much to do. You have only so much energy, so much time, so many resources. There is only so much you can do in life.

Taking care of the needs of the membership *is* an important responsibility of the pastor. We *do* need to nurture our faithful Catholics and to strengthen them in their faith through myriad pastoral activities, such as the liturgy, religious education, pastoral visits, and counseling. So what's wrong with that? Our task is *also* to nurture them in the faith so that *they* become active disciples and disciple-makers, not "consumer Catholics." An essential part of our nurturing is to equip *them* to carry out the mission and ministry of Jesus in a community of disciples called the Church.

Next—*why* should we move from maintenance-to mission-oriented parishes? First of all, we need to do so because Jesus said so. Most people are familiar with the bracelet that says *WWJD*, meaning, "What would Jesus do?" Well, it seems pretty clear from his words and actions in the gospels that Jesus would not be content to spend all his energy on the ninety-nine sheep in the fold. He explicitly said, "I have come for the lost sheep. Those who are well do not need the physician; the sick do." How much of Jesus's time and energy was spent defending his practice of reaching out and including those whom the authoritative religion of his day excluded? In some ways, one might say this issue of inclusion/exclusion helps explain why Jesus ended up on the cross.

Evangelization may have entered the Catholic consciousness again as a result of the Second Vatican Council, but evangelization did not begin with the council. It goes back to Jesus himself. Jesus created a missionary Church. *The Decree on the Church's Missionary Activity* tells us that the "Church on earth is by its very nature missionary" (*Ad Gentes* 2). In his magisterial work *Transforming Mission*, David Bosch says, "Without mission the church cannot be called catholic."[5] All the principal post–Vatican II documents that establish the foundations for a contemporary theology of evangelization make the point that evangelization goes back to Jesus himself. As Pope Paul VI tells us, Jesus is the "Good News of God" and the "first and the greatest evangelizer" (*Evangelii Nuntiandi* 2).

Furthermore, all the documents of the council reinforce the understanding that this missionary character is part of the whole Church, including all the baptized. All of us have a responsibility to proclaim the good news of the kingdom. Prior to the Second Vatican Council, if one inquired about who missionaries are and where the mission is, one would have received the answer that missionaries are the Jesuits, the White Fathers, and the Maryknoll priests and sisters, and that the missions are in Japan, Fiji, India, China, and Africa. Our post–Vatican II perspective tells us that the mission is wherever *we* are and that *we* are the missionaries.

I want to mention briefly two other very important reasons why we cannot content ourselves with being maintenance-oriented parishes. The first reason is obvious. There are 100 million people in the United States with no church family, 21 million of whom are inactive Catholics. Where are people who have no church family going to hear the good news in any convincing way? Many of them are spiritual in their orientation or even very religious in their personal practice, but they have no connection with the Church. Many of them draw their inspiration from religious television. But, of course, as Pope Paul VI pointed out long ago, one cannot separate adherence to Jesus Christ from belonging to a church family. The full gospel can only be lived out in community.

Among the 21 million inactive Catholics, there are countless numbers who need to hear an invitation from active Catholics because they feel unwanted, not missed, rejected, excluded, deeply alienated, or perhaps even excommunicated. How will they know they are missed unless we tell them? How will they know we care about them unless we show them? How will they know they are welcome back into their family of faith without a word from us? Unless our parishes become more mission-oriented, those 21 million inactive Catholics may well go elsewhere for their spiritual nourishment. This is happening in alarming proportions in the Hispanic community and among many religious seekers who do not feel they are being nourished in the Catholic Church. If Catholic parishes don't begin to focus their energies on the millions of people within their parish boundaries who have no church family, we will have failed miserably in the one thing that we should be about as Church.

Many people will recall many less-than-satisfying homilies about the Mary-Martha story in the gospels. I would like to offer a communal interpretation of that passage, one that challenges our Catholic parishes to stop being busy about many things and get focused on the one thing that really matters. When are we going to get serious about carrying out the mandate we have received from Christ? When are we going to get about the Lord's business? I would rather fail at the one right thing than have a lot of success in something that does not matter at all to the Lord!

There is one additional reason for moving from maintenance to mission, which I can only hint at here but have treated at some length in my book: the obstacles to evangelization. We are going through some difficult times being the Catholic Church right now. In addition to the painful and continuing sexual-abuse saga, we have the difficult aftermath of the implementation of the Second Vatican Council, which I have named a period of disorientation.[6] By that, I mean a period where we are struggling to come to a new equilibrium because our pre–Vatican II paradigm no longer fits. Certainly, this is what happened after the Second Vatican Council. It was a reform council, to use John O'Malley's term, and it challenged our whole way of being Church in many ways. It forced us to rethink and change the way we do things in many different areas. This caused a lot of confusion, displacement, tension, divisions, and disorientation that we are still working through.

I believe that becoming an evangelizing Church and moving from maintenance- to mission-oriented parishes can do an awful lot to bring healing in our present distress. It is easy to exaggerate and inflate our family and community problems when we don't have something outside of ourselves to bring perspective and a healthy sense of balance to our own troubles. We become absorbed by our problems. We engage in a feeding frenzy around our internal divisions and tensions. The Asian tsunami, Hurricane Katrina, and other national and international disasters illustrate very lucidly how we often find a new breadth of life in reaching out to those in distress. Things suddenly take on a new perspective. We have a new set of glasses with which to view our problems.

Without elaborating unduly on this point, I would simply say this: Evangelization is a very complex and profound reorientation of ourselves as Church. It can move us not only from maintenance to mission, but also from blindness to new levels of conversion, from excessive individualism to new-found solidarity, from fragmentation to deeper unity. Evangelization can be a healing balm for many of our current ills as a Church. To the degree that we stop focusing on ourselves and fix our eyes on Jesus, with a new intent to be faithful to the mission he has given to us, I believe we will be caught up in the goodness of that mission. We will also experience new satisfaction, healing, and joy in the way we ourselves are transformed.

John Paul II made this point, in effect, in *Mission of the Redeemer* (*Redemptoris Missio*), when he says that in evangelizing others, we ourselves are evangelized. "[For] missionary activity renews the Church, revitalizes faith and Christian identity, and offers fresh enthusiasm and new incentive. Faith is strengthened when faith is given away" (2). To put it another way, moving from maintenance to mission will bring new revitalization to parish life. How to do it is the second part of this essay.

How to Move from Maintenance to Mission

Now for the more difficult part: *How* do we make the move from maintenance to mission? At this point I need to remind all of us to think of ourselves as Tiger Woods. Some years ago, a commercial featured a number of people saying, "I am Tiger Woods. I am Tiger Woods." Well, let it be so. Let's all be Tiger Woods as we contemplate the challenge of moving from maintenance to missionary parishes, which will require of us both a considerable skill-package, such as Tiger Woods possesses, as well as the quality of being a grinder that I mentioned at the beginning of this article. Both will be necessary. Grinding alone won't do it. We need a new skill-set, a new way of "doing parish." But at the same time, as we acquire that new skill-set, we will need perseverance: a relentless and tenacious commitment to continue to give it our best shot, day in and day out, and to stay the course—qualities that Tiger Woods manifests in such exemplary fashion. The reason we will need these qualities is because moving from maintenance to missionary parishes is a long-term proposition and there are some serious obstacles.

What steps can we take to build enthusiasm and commitment for evangelization and to sharpen our desire to implement that vision of a Catholic parish and make it real in our local faith communities? Let me offer three very promising strategies.[7]

The first promising strategy came to mind when I was recently making a retreat. The spiritual director from the retreat house asked me how I related to God in my own personal spirituality. When we got to talking about Jesus, I told her that I related to Jesus as a disciple. She was rather surprised and wondered if I didn't think of Jesus as my friend. No, I like the notion that I am his disciple. It set me to wondering how people relate to that notion of themselves as disciples of Jesus. It is, of course, a very prominent metaphor from the gospels and has again grown in prominence in the Catholic Church since the Second Vatican Council, but it is not a dominant theme in Catholic spiritual life. Thomas Rausch, SJ, makes the point that the classic medieval expression of discipleship was *The Imitation of Christ*. This devotional book, along with the Spiritual Exercises of St. Ignatius of Loyola, best represents a Catholic spirituality of discipleship that gives preeminence to following Jesus and living according to gospel values.[8] Many years ago, when Avery Dulles published his expanded version of *Models of the Church*, he added the Church as a "Community of Disciples" because it was an inclusive model that had great potential for a comprehensive ecclesiology.

So how do people relate to that term? Does the image of themselves as a disciple of Christ have a positive connotation for them? What feelings do they have when they think of themselves as a disciple of Jesus Christ?

Thinking of ourselves as a community of disciples is a first, promising strategy for moving from maintenance to mission and transforming the way we "do church." First of all, a disciple, as the word suggests, is primarily a learner—indeed, a lifelong learner. Imagine a Catholic parish in which more and more people see themselves as lifelong learners. As a Christian, I never graduate from the school of formation.

Furthermore, I realize that as a Christian I am a work in progress. At every stage of life I need to find new ways of seeing myself in Christ to meet the challenge of the particular stage of the journey where I am. My childhood formation in the faith is not going to get me through the challenges of adult life.

The *General Directory of Catechesis* points out that a critical aspect of the formation of disciples is fostering a vital relationship with Christ. A disciple is someone who, first of all, is in relationship with the person of Christ. A personal relationship with Christ is the good soil upon which growth in knowledge of the content of the faith can take place.[9] "The fundamental task of catechesis is, therefore, to form disciples of Christ and to send them forth in mission."[10] This has enormous implications for our ongoing spiritual formation as Catholic Christians. We are on a journey with Christ. We are following Christ through the various stages of our life experience. This way of thinking of ourselves as baptized Christians can help us overcome a major obstacle to Catholic evangelization: inactive Catholics and people with no church family have the perception that Catholics have a religion but not a spirituality. They *see* that Catholics have priests, laws, structures, institutions, sacraments, and rituals, but where is the spirituality? Where is the personal relationship?

Coming to see ourselves as a community of disciples can nurture the kind of spirituality within the Church that will help counteract that perception. It makes the Church—and us Catholics—more attractive to those who are looking in from outside. Religion will be attractive to them only if it can offer them a spirituality for their lives. Thinking of ourselves and modeling ourselves from the beginning as a community of disciples can do a great deal to feed people's spiritual hungers—both those of us who are within the Church and those who are not.

One final word about the metaphor of a disciple. A disciple is someone who lives in a relationship of dependence on Christ, the teacher and master. A person can't be a faithful disciple if he or she doesn't pay attention to what the master says and does. The magisterium is a prominent part of our Catholicism. So the Church is very comfortable being a teaching Church. But we are a little short on being a learning Church. This past year we celebrated the fortieth anniversary of the promulgation of the *Dogmatic Constitution on Divine Revelation (Dei Verbum)*. That great document reminds us that the "Magisterium is not superior to the word of God, but is rather its servant. It teaches only what has been handed on to it. At the divine command and with the help of the Holy Spirit, it listens to this devoutly, guards it reverently and expounds it faithfully" (10).

What will happen to us as a Church if we continue to listen faithfully to the Word of God in Jesus Christ? We will not be able to ignore his command to go and make disciples of all nations. Nor will we be able to ignore the example he set for us as the first evangelizer, who constantly reached out to people on the margins and sought those who were lost. In summary, we cannot be a Church that is a community of disciples if we don't listen to the word of the master. The Lord Jesus is calling us to create missionary parishes.

A second promising strategy for any parish trying to move from maintenance to mission is to concentrate on becoming more welcoming *and* more inviting. Obviously, the two go hand in hand, for unless we are a welcoming parish, we have nothing attractive to invite people to. Parishes have discovered, in fact, that one of the best ways to become more evangelizing is to become more welcoming. Whether changing the atmosphere at our Sunday Eucharist, or becoming more effective at greeting and receiving newcomers, or transforming the physical facilities to make them more user-friendly and inclusive—efforts to become more welcoming have met with great success. We must continue along that path. Carrie Kemp, in her book *Catholics Can Come Home Again*, offers a model-parish welcoming checklist that parishes can use to monitor their progress in this important area.[11]

Let me say something about this welcoming effort—something that shows how challenging it really is. Welcoming cannot be equated with simply becoming more friendly. To be a parish that is friendly only to its own kind is not the model of the welcoming parish we are talking about. Welcoming is about becoming, first all, more inclusive, more accepting of people, no matter their color, race, ethnic origin, language, social status, or sexual orientation.

When I was pastor of our Paulist parish in Los Angeles, I spent a great deal of time talking to a man named Silver. Silver was part Native American, part Mexican, and full-time alcoholic and resident of the street. He had spent seventeen years in prison for murdering a man. Our conversations always took place in the gathering area at the back of the church. Silver didn't feel worthy to go inside the church because

93

he couldn't forgive himself for killing another human being. But there was another reason why Silver didn't come into the church. He felt that the people in the parish didn't think he belonged there, either. He didn't feel welcome. So he stayed outside the church and died on the streets of Los Angeles. Welcoming is not about being friendly to your own; it is about becoming a Church that opens itself to all God's people.

So one side of the equation is to become more welcoming. The other, equally challenging, side is to take the risk of becoming more inviting. This is an area where we Catholics can grow a lot. I once was speaking to a seventy-five-year-old gentleman in the Midwest, who told me that he had just come into the Church. I jokingly asked him why he waited so long. He said, "Nobody ever invited me." Then he told me that his son was a Catholic priest.

Now, let's go back to those 21 million inactive Catholics in this country, who feel totally unwanted by the Church. Only a specific and sincere invitation from us will let them know that we miss them and we want them back in the family. I had a high school classmate who married a Jewish woman and raised his two children in the Jewish faith. Years later he began to explore his Catholic roots. However, he was under the impression that he couldn't come back because what he had done irrevocably closed the doors of the Church to him. I had to help him understand that those doors were still open.

Today, it is very exciting to realize that Catholics are becoming less and less reluctant to reach out and invite. There are many signs that we are overcoming our shyness. I am from Minnesota, the land of the chosen, frozen people. We don't talk much in Minnesota, as anyone who has seen the movie *Fargo* knows: "Yup," "Nope," and "You betcha" are the holy trinity of Minnesota-speak. But even in Minnesota, Catholic hearts are beginning to thaw and Catholic lips are issuing invitations.

Some years ago, as dioceses were finishing *Disciples in Mission*, which is the Paulist National Catholic Evangelization Association's formation process for evangelization, they asked for resources to help their churches become more inviting. We had nothing to offer them at that time. I am happy to report that the situation has changed. Recently, PNCEA—as the Association is more widely known—came out with two new brochures that can be given to people with no church family. One is called *Come and See*, part of a new resource called

Invite! The other is *We Miss You,* a brochure for inactive Catholics that is part of a new resource called *Catholics Reaching Out.* These provide some concrete help for parishes that are seeking innovative and effective ways to reach out to people.

Third, and this is perhaps the most challenging of the promising strategies, parishes trying to move from maintenance to mission need to grow in a collaborative style of ministry. Why is this important? Because this style of ministry is the best way for a parish to effectively choose and implement its evangelizing priorities. When a parish knows itself as a community of disciples and all its members have gifts to share, then those members are willing to take responsibility for the identity, character, and direction of parish life. And this includes evangelization.

The inertia of parish life is toward maintenance. If we don't consciously do something to change our way of doing parish, we will instinctively move toward the maintenance mode. It is, to use today's computer language, the default position of every parish. In order to move beyond maintenance, we need to become intentional about our evangelizing priorities.

Parishes are already busy places—too busy. Many parishes operate on the principle that more is better. Pastors are overwhelmed because they are often taking care of two or even three parishes. Unless we find a way to become more collaborative, and get widespread participation in the direction-setting and implementation of our priorities, we will default to that maintenance setting. The same people in the parish will keep doing everything and nothing will change. There will be no energy for outreach because there will be no new bodies to carry it out.

Gallup tells us that 57 percent of the people who volunteer for work in parishes are not using their gifts; they are merely filling slots. If we can find a way to turn our parish priorities over to people who have the passion to get them done and who have the gifts to bring to the task, we will be more successful in getting results. Just as important, we will create a high level of satisfaction among our parishioners, because they will feel they are making a difference. They will be working on priorities they believe in and they will be using their gifts to get the task accomplished.

Parishes that engage in a collaborative style of ministry move from maintenance to mission in the following ways:

- They engage people in shared decision-making processes that heighten parishioners' participation level because they have some say in the overall direction of the parish.
- They overcome the inertia toward maintenance by engaging in some kind of pastoral planning process that enables them to consciously choose evangelizing priorities.
- They elicit higher levels of parishioner involvement by engaging people according to their gifts, rather than by simply filling volunteer slots.
- They get results by turning to people who have the desire, passion, energy, and gifts to get things done—forming new "priority action groups," rather than depending on already existing committees.

Many parishes are reluctant to undertake new evangelizing initiatives because the pastor is already overworked, there is too much going on the parish, and there are no more volunteers to carry out these new tasks. What we don't always realize is that there are many people in our parishes who are just waiting to participate if we can find new ways to engage them. We must involve them, from the very beginning, in setting parish priorities, and we must invite the people who have the gifts and the passion for those priorities to carry them out.

PNCEA has developed such a planning process, called ENVISION. My brother-in-law is a longtime, very active leader in his parish. He reported that he knew the parish had been enormously successful in its efforts to engage parishioners through ENVISION when he saw that 75 percent of the people who had volunteered to carry out the newly identified priority actions were people whose names were unknown to him. Whatever the process we use, we need one that is truly collaborative, mission-focused, and Christ-centered that will get us similar results.

My purpose in this article has been to add flame to the fire of the Spirit that already burns in us, to challenge us to continue our work of carrying on the reform of the Second Vatican Council, and to offer some specific strategies that can enable every one of our parishes to move from maintenance to mission—and to revitalization. Let's keep the evangelizing flames burning!

NOTES

1. Pope John Paul II, "Mission: The Right and Duty of Every Christian," Papal Message for World Mission Day, October 20, 1991.

2. Frank DeSiano and Kenneth Boyack, *Creating the Evangelizing Parish* (Mahwah, NJ: Paulist Press, 1993), 86–91.

3. *Code of Canon Law, Latin-English Edition* (Washington, DC: Canon Law Society of America, 1983), Canon 528.

4. Patrick Brennan, *Re-Imagining the Parish* (New York: Crossroad, 1991), 10.

5. David J. Bosch, *Transforming Mission: Paradigm Shifts in Theology of Mission* (Maryknoll, NY: Orbis Books, 1996), 372.

6. This term is borrowed from Walter Brueggemann, based upon an earlier work of Paul Ricoeur.

7. These are not meant to be exhaustive. Other promising strategies include offering awakening experiences, fostering small faith-sharing communities, and adopting an evangelizing perspective on all parish activities.

8. *New Dictionary of Catholic Spirituality*, ed. Michael Downey (Collegeville, MN: The Liturgical Press, 1993), 281–84.

9. *General Directory for Catechesis* (Washington, DC: United States Conference of Catholic Bishops, 1997), 16.

10. *Leader's Guide to the National Directory for Catechesis* (Washington, DC: United States Conference of Catholic Bishops, 2005), 53.

11. Carrie Kemp, *Catholics Can Come Home Again: A Guide for the Journey of Reconciliation with Inactive Catholics* (Mahwah, NJ: Paulist Press, 2001), 75–77.

8

A Pastor's Response to "From Maintenance to Mission"

Marc Montminy

As I formulate my response to Fr. Robert Rivers' chapter "From Maintenance to Mission: Evangelization and the Revitalization of the Parish," I find myself reflecting on this foundational truth: Evangelization is the crown jewel of the Church.

Introduction

I am going to begin with a bold statement: Most of us who are ordained as priests and deacons do not have a clue as to what evangelization is and how to go about sharing the good news of Jesus Christ with others. Institutional Catholicism has done a wonderful job of writing and publishing documents, but a poor job in evangelizing and catechizing the average person in the pew.

The years after Vatican II have turned out to be a period in Church history when a reaction to issues has proven to be more important than truth. We have come a long way, but the American Church is being challenged to change the mindset that made it successful in previous times and to reorient its language, mission, and approach in the twenty-first century.

I know that most priests, who happen to be the leaders of a vast majority of parishes across the United States, may not even realize that their mode of ministry is one of maintenance rather than mission. Our language, our training, and our approach have been inadequate. Seminaries never trained their prospective priests with techniques or methodology that dealt with mission and/or vision.

Indeed, the typical parish in the Northeast continues to use a model in which ministry is seen as the priest "saying Mass" and the laity engaged in such "jobs" as pastoral ministers, youth ministers, and religious education coordinators or directors. Ministry is seen to be the area given over to those who distribute communion, who are lectors or who greet at the door of the church.

The average parish in America deals with a passive spectator community—one that, for the most part, has not understood that the scriptures used at liturgy are the Word of God and one that still is uncertain as to whether the bread and wine consecrated by the priest really is the Body and Blood of Christ or whether the Eucharist is the source and summit of Catholic life.

We baptize babies of parents who make empty professions of faith and who see the sacraments as something that is owed to them. We teach CCD to children who have not been evangelized. We use techniques that ignore, for the most part, the media and the multifaceted approach to education in which most of our children are engaged from morning till night. We confirm young people who go through the motions of the sacrament without consenting to the power of the Holy Spirit. Does some of this work? Certainly it does. We still have many parishes across the country that are full on Sundays and where the gospel is truly lived out. However, there are just as many parishes that are empty.

In recent years, priests have been "brainwashed" into thinking that we are an overworked and aging group and that we have nothing left to do but to maintain the status quo and wait for some miracle to happen. The entire focus of the conversation at most presbytery meetings is on maintenance: How do we care for ourselves? What about retirement and benefits? How much more work can we take on? Some have even resorted into thinking that, if we wait long enough, we may be able to move the clock backward and experience the good old days. Canon 528 regarding the pastoral duty to care for all the souls that dwell within one's parish boundary has never been mentioned in most seminaries.

If bishops acted as quickly on implementing documents on evangelization as they did during the sexual-abuse crisis, I believe that we would be in a very different place today. Over 21 million inactive Catholics should evoke a response in all of us to the call to evangelize. If we continue to be self-absorbed as a Church, we will never be able to get out of the way and let God work with the power of the Holy Spirit.

Fr. Rivers' Article

Fr. Rivers has done us a great favor in addressing so clearly the necessity of living out the great commandment to "Go and make disciples." As the pastor of a large inner-city parish with great needs, Fr. Rivers has challenged me personally to strive wholeheartedly and with greater zeal to build up the kingdom of God by refocusing all aspects of the parish through the prism of evangelization. I have taken his message to heart and believe that what he is presenting to us is revolutionary. An evangelizing revolution is needed in the Church!

I would like to reiterate the central thesis of Fr. Rivers' presentation. In describing the maintenance-oriented parish, he defines it as an inward-looking parish, focused on the everyday needs of making the parish machinery work. There is a sense of going through the motions just to get things done. Overburdened by this, the maintenance-oriented parish succumbs to "focusing solely on its current members, who absorb most of its time, energy, and resources." Evangelization thus becomes an item on a list of things to do when the pastor has the time.

The mission-oriented parish, on the other hand, is one that looks outward and sees the souls that are in need of care, love, and forgiveness. It involves the active life of the Holy Spirit by incorporating the necessary atmosphere of openness by welcoming and inviting people to come and see, by having a deliberate sense of pastoral purpose and goals, by making decisions that are inspired, and by using the spiritual and personal gifts of its members. In this way not only is the gospel being made alive, but through the spiritual and corporal works of mercy the kingdom of God is being built. People from all walks of life experience the incarnation and become true disciples. In fact, there is a sense of the prophetic in the mission-oriented parish.

A Staff Discussion of Fr. Rivers' Article

I was able to share Fr. Rivers' article with my parish staff. We met for an entire day of reflection and used the article as basis for our discussion. The parish staff is comprised of two full-time religious education coordinators, a full-time youth minister, two full-time evangelists and one part-timer, a pastoral minister, and the parish priests. Thus, this group comprised the ministerial activity in the parish that ranges from children and youth to the elderly, from the hospital bed to the homebound and the nursing home, from the poor on our streets to the family in the pew, from religious education of the youth to the religious education of the adults, and from Bible study to the sacramental and liturgical ministries.

The Crown Jewel

As we began our discussion, we felt that the ability to relate to Jesus as a disciple was pivotal. This is a foundational element of evangelization and perhaps the tie that binds the crown jewel of the Church in place. The message of the good news—salvation, healing, forgiveness, and eternal life with the God who is love—needs to be made known before discipleship can flourish. Kerygma, *proclaiming* the good news, is the cornerstone of discipleship: sharing our relationship with Jesus so that others may come to know him fully in his incarnation, teachings, miracles, passion, death, resurrection, and ultimate return.

Upon reflection, staff members realized that many people in the Church, including ourselves, base the concept of evangelization either on some sort of proselytizing or solely on people coming to know about Jesus. We acknowledge that many of our Evangelical brothers and sisters do a much better job of sharing the good news than we do. We can learn from them that kerygma is not something to be just studied in a book or document but experienced through a community that is mission-oriented. In other words, Jesus is a real person and our personal relationship with him must be transformed into discipleship.

The Model of Christ and the Saints

Bear with me as I recall a story of one of the great missionaries and evangelists in the life of the Church, St. Francis Xavier. The story takes place while Francis was in Nagasaki, Japan, in the seventeenth century. It was the time of the great warlords—the shoguns—whose own missionaries were comprised of the samurai. Francis made it his custom to sit in the town center each day and pray his Divine Office. Many of the people who were attracted to his presence took catechism from him, learned about Jesus, and were baptized. So the warlord sent his samurai to confront the priest.

The samurai, in full and magnificent armor, towered over Francis. He looked down and stated, "Priest, if you do not tell me what heaven and hell are, you will surely die in this place." Francis looked up from his breviary and responded in a plain voice to the samurai, "You are very stupid." Rage filled the samurai, and he raised his *katana*—his sword—to strike the priest. Francis looked up again and said, "Not only are you stupid, but you are also very ugly." The wrath of the samurai increased a hundredfold and he raised his other sword. Now both arms were raised up, ready to strike the priest dead. Francis continued to look in the warrior's eyes and, seeing his rage and anger, said, "Now you know what hell is like." His words were like a lance that pierced the samurai's armor straight to the heart. His arms fell to his side, his swords fell to the ground, and his knees buckled. The priest, now face to face with the warrior, looked once more into the eyes of the man and said, "Now you know what heaven is like."

I share this story with you because Fr. Rivers explicitly states that, as a Church, we are accustomed to thinking that evangelization is strictly the domain of the "hero priest." I recall many stories of those priests, from the apostles to Augustine of Canterbury, from Boniface and Patrick to the North American martyrs, whose blood was spilled for the gospel. We do not have the luxury of relying solely on the great missionary religious communities like Maryknoll, the Paulists, the Jesuits, and countless others for our evangelizing efforts. However, there is a great need for the sacrificial aspect that we learn from them in our mission-oriented parish. A little blood, sweat, and toil will get us a long way, and we should not be afraid of a little sacrifice. The disciple, as Jesus said, should "pick up the cross and follow me."

From Discipleship to Evangelist

During my meeting with the parish staff, we discovered the great need to restructure all of our ministries on the foundation of evangelization through sharing the good news and building up discipleship. After we had a good period of discussion based on Fr. Rivers' article, we decided that the best means to accomplish this was in two ways: conversion and prophetic ministry. We came to these two points in a roundabout way: we were complaining about the diocese.

Most dioceses are the same. Our complaints were centered on, among other things, the bureaucracy, the paperwork, the "disconnect" between the parishes and the diocesan leadership, and the lack of ministerial assistance. This, coupled with what Fr. Rivers realistically calls "the obstacles to evangelization," such as the priest scandals of the past few years, led us to the conclusion that not only have parishes become maintenance-oriented but so too has the diocesan administration. Let me share an example of what is occurring in my own diocese.

Currently we are heavily involved in planning the future of the diocese, as are most other dioceses. This futuristic planning is centered on the closing of parishes. Although it is true that some of the inner-city parishes must be closed due to a lack of residents, the main reasons behind the mergers and closings are a projected lack of priests, and, at times, a lack of money. What is also occurring, however, is the closing of parishes in smaller communities. This lack of Catholic identity in these rural towns is devastating. As the maintenance-oriented parish looks inward and stops any missionary work, so does the diocese. I believe that we are on the wrong track. We should be looking not at the priest shortage to determine which parishes to close; instead, we should be looking at the needs of God's people. This is the revolution that I previously mentioned. In our work of evangelization, we should not be dwelling on the priesthood; we should be considering the needs of God's people. I forgot which saint said this, but it applies here: "If we look only at ourselves, we soon become depressed. If we turn our gaze to God, we will soon find joy." This holds true not just for the individual, but also for the parish and the diocese.

The reality of the situation hits home whenever we orient our gaze toward the maintenance mode. As Catholics, we have not done a very good job at changing the attitude among both the clergy and the laity toward the grace of being disciples and of being a people who welcome and share the good news. At this point we, as a staff, came up with two points that describe mission-oriented parishes and dioceses: conversion and prophecy.

Conversion

Our complaining about the diocese lasted only a few moments. Suddenly, we felt that *we* needed conversion for complaining so much. We, the parish, needed to turn our gaze to Jesus Christ. It had to begin with the staff, ministers, and everyday churchgoers.

Sacred Scripture reminds us that each and every encounter that people had with Jesus involved either the call to conversion or a moment of conversion. We have to remember only the story of Zacchaeus, who climbed a tree to see Jesus, or the call of Matthew Levi when we think about biblical conversion stories. Why did Jesus make them, and countless others, his disciples? The answer becomes clear when we remember that Jesus said he came to find the lost and that the sick need doctors. He also reminded us that we need to learn that he desires mercy and not sacrifice. In our parishes and in our streets today, the names may be different but the needs are the same. The mission-oriented parish must be a converted parish. It needs to see its own weaknesses, attitudes, obstacles, and even sins, and then repent of them, turn away from them, and be faithful to the gospel.

Fr. Rivers mentions some of the typical obstacles that the parish in need of conversion encounters. Besides the more publicized bishops' and priests' scandals, there are two that are prominent: First, the attitude that "We are already overworked and we don't have the time or energy." Second, the attitude that "It is someone else's job." This reflects a very modern American attitude, which I call "comfortitis." As a people and as a Church in this country, we have been so comfortable that we have lost the missionary zeal of our ancestors. We feel that if we have people coming to Mass, it is enough. We take our people's faith for granted. They are searching and knocking at the door so that faith, hope, and love will be opened to them. They need to experience what we say at Mass is true—that Jesus will come to complete our joy.

I would like to share another story. This example of discipleship and welcoming is drawn from the Franciscan tradition.

> I, [Francis] return from Perugia and arrive here in the dead of night; and it is winter time, muddy and so cold that icicles have formed on the edges of my habit and keep striking my legs, and blood flows from such wounds. And all covered with mud and cold, I come to the gate and after I have knocked and called for some time, a brother comes and asks: "Who are you?" I answer: "Brother Francis." And he says: "Go away; this is not a proper hour for going about; you may not come in."
>
> And when I insist, he answers: "Go away, you are a simple and stupid person; we are so many and we have no need of you. You are certainly not coming to us at this hour!" And I stand again at the door and say: "For the love of God, take me in tonight." And he answers: "I will not. Go to the Crosiers' place and ask there."
>
> I tell you this: If I had patience and did not become upset, there would be true joy in this and true virtue and the salvation of the soul.[1]

Our people, like Francis, are standing at the door waiting for us to open it and invite them in. Again, the needs of God's people are the same today as when Jesus called his first disciples. There is the need for hope, for forgiveness, for healing, for belonging, for invitation, for revealing, for learning, for compassion, for worshipping, for food, for clothing, for shelter, and, above all, the need for giving and for receiving love. The converted mission-oriented parish bases its evangelization on the needs of God's children and brings about the good news through the corporal and spiritual works of mercy. We can never be too overworked to be charitable and we can never wait for someone else to come along and be compassionate. If we don't answer the door, they will go and knock on another door and wait for the invitation to enter.

Prophecy

Prophecy? Let me explain.

Fr. Rivers pointed out that the mission-oriented parish uses the gifts of its people. Reflecting on St. Paul's list of ministries in 1 Corinthians, we find the following description of gifts in the Body of Christ:

> Now there are varieties of gifts, but the same Spirit; and there are varieties of services, but the same Lord; and there are varieties of activities, but it is the same God who activates all of them in everyone. To each is given the manifestation of the Spirit for the common good. To one is given through the Spirit the utterance of wisdom, and to another the utterance of knowledge according to the same Spirit, to another faith by the same Spirit, to another gifts of healing by the one Spirit, to another the working of miracles, to another prophecy, to another the discernment of spirits, to another various kinds of tongues, to another the interpretation of tongues. All these are activated by one and the same Spirit, who allots to each one individually just as the Spirit chooses. (1 Cor 12:4–11)

The giftedness of the mission-oriented parish is focused not on its many ministries but instead on the Holy Spirit, the Living Spirit, and the Spirit of God, who grants all these gifts and *who has spoken to us through the prophets.* My staff constantly reminds me that not only are we all baptized to be priests and kings, but, like Christ, we are all baptized to be prophets. A prophet is someone who reveals God, his will, his way, his love, and his mercy. The prophet is not afraid of hardship or even mockery. Often the prophet fails. However, the instrument of the prophet is simple, easy, and light: It is the "invitation."

Two recent experiences remind me of the commitment that we need repeatedly to invite people to *come and see.* Fr. Rivers, I believe, makes this the key to evangelization. The first experience comes from our "Theology on Tap" series. Two parishioners came up to me and we began to talk. I asked them if they were going to come the next night to our monthly men-only eucharistic adoration sponsored by the Men of St. Joseph. They said that they have never heard of it—even after I had just announced it at all the Sunday Masses, and we have been doing it for years. They had to be personally invited to *come and see*. I had to open the door for them to find Christ.

That same week, I received a phone call from another parishioner. He told me that he felt called to serve the poor in the parish, and asked why we didn't have anything going on for the poor in the parish. I was a little dumbfounded that he didn't know about our St. Vincent de Paul store, St. Vincent de Paul food bank, People Helping People program, active campaign to assist a missionary priest and society in the Appalachia region of Kentucky, groups of eucharistic ministers who bring communion to shut-ins and nursing homes every Sunday, and countless other ministries. It was his turn to be dumbfounded as a weekly attendee at Mass. He said that he never heard of these ministries. So I personally invited him to join the St. Vincent de Paul Society and to attend an upcoming Cursillo. Again, he said that he had never heard of Cursillo. Yet, one of my associates and I have been involved in it for twenty years!

Even though we put all these activities and ministries in the bulletin and announce them from the pulpit, such things go in one ear and out the other. The prophetic "invitation" seems to be the missing element and the medicine for converting a maintenance-oriented parish into a mission-oriented parish.

Conclusion: The Personal Invitation to Come and See Is the Key to Evangelization

At the conclusion of our staff meeting, the question was raised: "How do we implement this instrument of the mission-oriented parish in our own parish?" One member, searching for inspiration to solve our dilemma, mentioned the axiom KISS: "Keep It Simple Stupid!" Another brought up "Occam's Razor," which states that "all else being equal, the simpler theory is more preferable." In response, someone finally concluded that those expressions were just complicated versions of what the great fictional detective Sherlock Holmes used to say to his dear friend Dr. Watson: "It's elementary!" In the most revolutionary and simplistic description of evangelization, I proclaim to you that every member of the parish needs to invite God's people at all times, and that as ministers, we need to practice it ourselves and teach others to do the same.

I suggest to you that the following methods be used to do this:

❏ Pray the Holy Spirit for a fresh outpouring.
❏ Embrace new and revolutionary models needed in the Church:
  • The bishops' conference needs to meet and pray for greater vision and conversion.
  • Parishes need to pray for conversion and openness to new and integral ways of inviting, welcoming, and sharing the gospel with people.
  • Movements are needed that lead people to encounter Christ.
  • Baptism in the Holy Spirit, Cursillo, Engaged Encounter, Marriage Encounter, and other such methods of inviting people to encounter Christ should become normative.
❏ Embrace the cross, ask for God's mercy, and seek above all the glory of God.

As I come to the conclusion of my response to Fr. Rivers' article, I need to express my appreciation for both it and for my staff. We promised that we would move forward through our own obstacles and those of our parishioners in order not to settle into maintenance-mode but to rely on the power of the Holy Spirit to bring the good news of Jesus to all through kerygma, discipleship, and prophetic action.

NOTE

1. Marion A. Habig, ed., *St. Francis of Assisi: Writings and Early Biographies* (Chicago, IL: Franciscan Herald Press, 1973), 1318–20.

9

A Study of Hispanic Catholics: Why Are They Leaving the Catholic Church?

Implications for the New Evangelization

Edwin Hernández
with Rebecca Burwell and Jeffrey Smith

When Pope John Paul II lifted up his vision for a "New Evangelization in the Americas," he spoke of the need for the universal gospel of Christ to be inculturated when presented "to a particular people" (*Ecclesia in America* 70). The Holy Father's summons to a renewed proclamation of the faith invoked the *"mestiza* face of the Virgin of Guadalupe," who, he noted, "was from the start a symbol of the inculturation of the Gospel, of which she has been the lodestar and the guide" (ibid.).

For most Anglo-Catholics in the United States, the image of Nuestra Señora is still something of a novelty. Though the Catholic faith found a home in the Central and Southern American peoples some five centuries ago, recent immigration patterns are now reconstructing the face of the Catholic Church north of the border. The challenge and opportunity of this demographic shift is particularly pronounced in parts of the country where Latino/as are relative newcomers, and where communities are wrestling with how to respond to the rising prominence of Latino/as[1] in their midst. To heed John Paul II's summons to evangelization, the Catholic Church in the United States will need to pay careful attention to the population that will soon account for 40 percent of it members.

Ministering in the American context is further complicated by the growing appeal of Evangelical and Pentecostal Protestantism, both at home and abroad. Though Latino/as have historically found their Christian home in the Catholic Church, for some their geographic relocation is paralleled by an equivalent denominational move. But though this trend toward religious conversion, or "switching" as sociologists call it, has received much attention over the past twenty years (Greeley 1988, Greeley 1997, Hunt 1998, Hernández 1999), both the extent and the causes of Latino/a conversion to Protestantism remain contested. This paper draws upon current research and theory to explore the dynamics of the Latino/a presence within the Catholic Church in the United States, the trends concerning religious switching from Catholicism to Protestantism, and key opportunities for a Catholic response.

Latino/as in the United States

It is hardly a secret that at 42.7 million, Latino/as are now the largest minority group in the United States.[2] With continued (im)migration, a higher birth rate,[3] and a comparatively young population,[4] the impact of Latino/a culture on the broader society in the United States is only going to increase in the years ahead. As Table 1 shows, U.S. Census predictions estimate a 166 percent growth in Latino/a population in the United States over the next forty-five years, by which time Latino/as will make up nearly a quarter of the entire population.

Much of this growth is due to immigration. The Pew Hispanic Center reports that in 2005, there were 37.4 million foreign-born individuals living in the United States, of which nearly 8.7 million were unauthorized immigrants from Latin America (5.9 million from Mexico alone). But though the number of immigrants from Latin America has increased over the past two decades, recent analysis of immigration trends has found that the immigration rates have not been consistent

Table 1. Hispanic Population in the United States

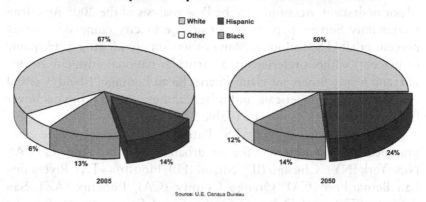

Source: U.S. Census Bureau

(Passel and Suro 2005). A steady growth of immigration during the nineties and a spike in 2001 paralleled the economic fortunes that the United States enjoyed at those times. The slight upturn in 2004–2005 to approximately 1.2 million incoming immigrants suggests a continued, albeit slow, increase in the number of immigrants who will cross the border in the years ahead.

Though considerable variation exists within the U.S.-Latino/a community, Latino/as as a group are poorer and have less access to social and civic resources than the non-Hispanic white population. In 2003 only 57 percent of Latino/as over twenty-five had a high school diploma, and only 30 percent had any college education (Stoops 2004). By comparison, 89 percent of non-Hispanic whites had graduated from high school, and 56 percent had completed some college (Stoops 2004). Foreign-born Latino/as were significantly less likely to have some college education than their United States–born equivalents— 22 percent vs. 40 percent, respectively (Stoops 2004).

The 2004 median household income for Latino/as ($34,241) was 30 percent lower than it was for non-Hispanic white households (U.S. Census Bureau 2004),[5] and 22 percent of Latino/as live below the poverty level compared to 9 percent of whites (U.S. Census Bureau 2004). Latino/a families are also larger and younger than the general population. The average Latino/a household has 3.6 members compared to 2.6 for the general population, and nearly 50 percent of Latino/as are under the age of eighteen. Despite their low earnings, 46 percent of foreign-born Latino/as send significant monetary remittances to their families in their home countries (Pew Hispanic Center 2005).

111

The vast majority of Latino/as in the United States are of Mexican descent. According to the Pew analysis of the 2005 American Community Survey, persons of Mexican ethnicity comprise over 64 percent of all U.S. Latino/as. Many others simply identify as Hispanic (7 percent) without referencing a particular national ethnicity or origin, and nearly 9 percent claim Puerto Rican heritage. Island, Central American, South American, and other Latino/a national origins hover between 3 and 7 percent each (Table 2).

The vast majority of U.S. Latino/as (88 percent) live geographically concentrated in the ten urban areas of Los Angeles (CA), New York (NY), Chicago (IL), Miami (FL), Houston (TX), Riverside–San Bernardino (CA), Orange County (CA), Phoenix (AZ), San Antonio (TX), and Dallas (TX) (Suro and Singer 2002). But the Latino/a population has been increasing outside of the Southwest and West coast as well. Data from the current population studies illustrates this: from 1990–2000 the Northwest saw a growth of 40 percent in its Latino/a population, the Midwest 81 percent, the West 52 percent, and the South 71 percent. In Michigan, the Latino/a population increased by 61 percent in this time period—a slightly higher rate than the national rate of 58 percent—which accounted for 19 percent of total population growth in the state. Latino/as comprise 3.7 percent of Wayne County (Detroit—5 percent), and 7 percent of Kent county (Grand Rapids—13.1 percent) (Andrade, Hernández, and Barberena-Medrano 2002).

Table 2. Latino/a Ethnicity in the United States

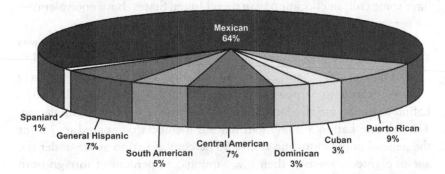

Spaniard 1%
General Hispanic 7%
South American 5%
Mexican 64%
Central American 7%
Dominican 3%
Cuban 3%
Puerto Rican 9%

Source: American Community Survey (Pew Analysis)

Though the presence of Latino/as is increasingly evident across the United States, Latino/as continue to live in predominantly minority neighborhoods. According to a 2005 study by the Pew Hispanic Center, 43 percent live in majority Latino/a communities commonly referred to as *barrios*, and another 7 percent live in predominantly African American neighborhoods. This same study found that while Latino/as are becoming geographically more dispersed, very few are moving to majority white neighborhoods.

Latino/a Catholics

Arriving from predominantly Catholic countries, Latino/as are the fastest growing segment of the Catholic Church in the United States. Estimates vary, but approximately 70 percent of U.S. Latino/as are Catholic.[6] Now estimated at 29.6 million individuals, Latino/as comprise as much as 37 percent of U.S. Catholics and are responsible for 71 percent of the growth in the U.S. Catholic population since 1960 (Perl et al. 2004). Like the general Latino/a population, Latino/a Catholics are young compared to the general population—nearly 50 percent are under the age of twenty.

The national origins of Latino/a Catholics mirror that of the general U.S. Latino/a population. According to the study "Hispanic Churches in American Public Life" (HCAPL) (Espinosa et al. 2003), the vast majority (73 percent) are of Mexican descent. As Table 3 shows, the remaining 27 percent are made up of Puerto Ricans (7 percent), Cubans (4 percent), Central Americans (10 percent), and South Americans (6 percent).

The Latino/a Catholic community includes a larger share of recent immigrants than does the Latino/a Protestant community. More than two-thirds (68 percent) of Latino/a Catholics were born outside of the United States, compared to 54 percent of Latino/a Protestants (Hernández 2006). Analysis of the Pew Hispanic Center's 2004 national survey of Latinos[7] shows that Latino/a Catholics also have a lower educational attainment rate than their Protestant equivalents. Only 28 percent of Latino/a Catholics have some college education, compared to 38 percent of Latino/a Protestants (Hernández 2006). Latino/a Catholics are also less acculturated than Latino/a

Table 3. Ethnic Identity by Religious Family

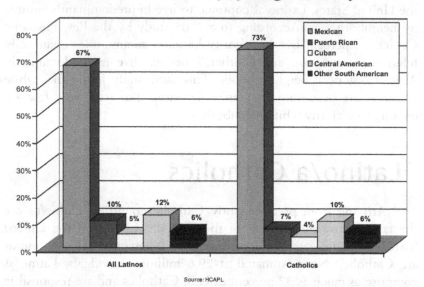

Source: HCAPL

Protestants—only 18 percent of Latino/a Catholics are English-language dominant compared to 35 percent of Latino/a Protestants (Hernández 2006). These findings suggest that language acquisition and length of time in the United States both contribute to this denominational education rate disparity.

In spite of the dire warnings predicting a massive Latino/a exodus from the Catholic Church to Protestantism (Greeley 1988), the proportion of U.S. Latino/as that identifies itself as Catholic has remained constant over the past twenty years at around 70 percent, due primarily to immigration and high birthrates. But despite their significant presence in the Catholic community, Latino/as are disproportionately represented among the parish leadership, clergy, and hierarchy of the institutional Church, as Table 4 illustrates.

As Table 4 shows, there is only one Latino priest for roughly every 10,000 Latino/a Catholics in the United States, and only one United States–born Latino priest for every 27,000 U.S.-born Latino/a Catholics. At these rates, both foreign- and United States–born Latino/as are less represented among their clergy than the laity in Europe (1:1,350), Asia (1:2,475), Africa (1:4,700), and Latin America (1:7,150) (Instituto Fe y Vida). Though a larger share (15 percent) of priests-in-training is Latino than the percent of Latinos in the current

Table 4. Latino/a Catholics in the United States

Percent of Catholic Church that is Latino/a[8]	**39%**
Percent of parishes with a majority Latino/a presence[9]	**21%**
Percent of Catholic priests who are Latino[10]	**9%**
Percent of seminarians who are Latino[11]	**15%**
Percent of priests ordained in 2002 who are Latino[12]	**15%**
Percent of priests who are U.S.-born Latinos[13]	**1%**
Ratio of priests per general U.S. Catholic population[14]	**1:1,375**
Ratio of U.S. Latino priests per U.S. Latino/a Catholic population[15]	**1:9,925**
Ratio of U.S.-born Latino priests per U.S.-born Latino/a Catholic population[16]	**1:27,000**
Ratio of U.S. bishops per general U.S. Catholic population[17]	**1:231,000**
Ratio of U.S. Latino bishops per U.S. Latino/a Catholic population[18]	**1:1 million**

pool of clergy (9 percent), this increase is still far outpaced by the growth rate of the U.S. Latino/a population.

The situation in the Midwestern United States mirrors that of the broader U.S. Catholic Church. Though the city of Chicago has one of the largest concentrations of both Latino/as (26 percent) (Andrade et al. 2002) and Latino/a Catholics in the United States, as of January 2005 the racial/ethnic background of active diocesan priests in Chicago shows a considerable disproportion. As Table 5 shows, only 4 percent are Latino.

The underrepresentation of Latino/as in the priesthood matters to Latino/a parishioners, the majority of whom have a strong preference for Latino/a leadership. The National Community on Latino Leadership survey found that 55 percent of Latino/a Catholics believe that Latino/a leaders better represent their values than non-Latino/as, and 62 percent feel that Latino/a leaders better reflect their views on important issues (Davis et al. 2005). Despite this clear preference, analysis of surveys performed by the Center for Applied Research of the Apostolate (CARA) found that Latino men (7 percent) are considerably less likely than non-Latinos (23 percent) to have considered entering the priesthood (Gray and Gautier 2005).

Many Catholic parishes and ministries have responded to the current and foreseeable shortage of Latino/a clergy by advancing the

Table 5. Racial/Ethnic Composition of Catholic Population and Active Diocesan Priests (Jan 2005)

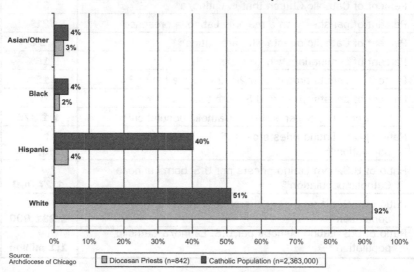

Source:
Archdiocese of Chicago

Diocesan Priests (n=842)   Catholic Population (n=2,363,000)

role of the laity in worship leadership. While this holds some promise, Latino/as currently comprise just 4 percent of professional lay ecclesial ministers in the Catholic Church (CARA).

As the information above reveals, the Latino/a Catholic Church in the United States is comprised largely of transplants. These immigrants and their progeny face challenges of acculturation and establishment, as well as economic and social hardships. While the Church remains one of the most consistent institutions in these newcomers' lives, the lack of Latino/a clergy and religious leaders makes it clear that non-Hispanic priests and lay leaders need to be better informed about the fastest growing sector of their community. To this end, the following section identifies the practices and commitments unique to Latino/a Catholics, and explores the influence on Latino/a Catholics in the United States made by Charismatic and Pentecostal movements both within and outside of the Church.

Latino/a Catholics in Action

The increasing proportion of Latino/as in the U.S.–Catholic Church requires careful engagement and understanding of the cultural differences between Latino/a expressions of faith and the European-American parishes that are becoming their homes. The combination of language and cultural differences often results in the Latino/a parishioners functioning as a kind of subgroup or subculture within the parish. Spanish Masses frequently are held separately from the larger community's regular worship services; in addition, the large presence of Charismatic Christian Renewal prayer-services within the Latino/a community has encouraged more autonomy and lay participation.

A survey conducted in 2000 found that 63 percent of active religious priests coming out of seminary felt inadequately prepared to work with multiple ethnic groups (Hoge 2002). To redress this situation, sociologist and Jesuit priest Allan Figueroa Deck suggests that the Catholic Church develop "leadership that is at once rooted in the particularity of the Latino/a cultures and faith traditions and rooted as well in the universality of the Catholic communion" (Deck 1998).

Father Deck's summons begs the question of what makes Latino/a Catholicism distinctive. Information gathered from the Chicago Latino Congregation Survey (CLCS)[19]—a landmark survey of Latino/a Catholic and Protestant Churches currently being conducted by the Center for the Study of Latino Religion at the University of Notre Dame—provides some important quantitative data to illuminate this question.

ATTENDANCE, RELIGIOSITY, AND DEVOTIONAL PRACTICES

Though Latino/as are often regarded as more "religious" than their Anglo-Catholic counterparts, findings from Robert Wuthnow's (2000) Religion and Politics survey indicate that only a slightly higher percent of Latino/as (61 percent) attend church regularly than non-Hispanic whites (58 percent). Among Latino/as, churchgoing behavior varies along denominational lines, with 77 percent of Latino/a Protestants attending church at least once a month in contrast to 64 percent of Latino/a Catholics.

Church attendance is only one of several ways to assess religious involvement and is not necessarily a good measure of Latino/a religiosity. Several scholars have noted that beyond parish worship life, Latino/as are more involved in prayer services, family devotions, and other religious practices such as celebrations of saints' days (Cadena 1995; D'Antonio et al. 2001; Peña and Freehill 1998). Young Latino/a Catholics are particularly engaged in these practices. Dean Hoge found that Latino/a Catholics under the age of thirty-five are more likely to offer weekly devotions to Mary or a special saint and to practice regular confession than those above thirty-five (Hoge 2001). In terms of the salience, or importance, of religion in Latino/as' daily lives, the HCAPL survey found that 61 percent of Latino/as say that religion is the "very to the most important" aspect of their lives and 53 percent say that religion provides "a great deal of guidance in their day to day living" (Espinosa et al. 2003).

COMMUNITY CONNECTEDNESS

For many Latino/as the Church is more than a place to worship. Sociologist Caleb Rosado has observed that Latino/a religious experience resembles a "*pueblo* both ethnic and communal, individual and social, a place not just for gathering individuals but bringing about a transcendent commonness" (Rosado 1995). Evidence for this lies in our finding that Latino/as are interconnected in their parishes, and have many close friends and family in the same congregation. Among Latino/a Catholics in our Chicago survey, 46 percent consider having friends and family in the parish one of the most attractive features of their congregations. This survey also found that only 30 percent of Catholics in Chicago attend a parish outside of their local boundaries, and 59 percent say that three or more of their five closest friends belong to the same parish.

SOCIAL JUSTICE AND INEQUALITY

The importance of the Church's social ministry is particularly relevant to the Latino/a community in light of their comparatively poor

Table 6. Has this church or someone from this church ever helped you or your family in the following ways?

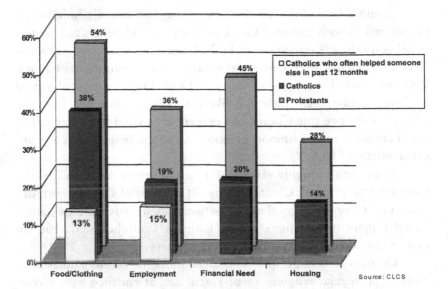

Source: CLCS

Legend:
- □ Catholics who often helped someone else in past 12 months
- ■ Catholics
- □ Protestants

Data (Food/Clothing): 13%, 38%, 54%
Data (Employment): 15%, 19%, 36%
Data (Financial Need): 20%, 45%
Data (Housing): 14%, 28%

socioeconomic status. In urban areas especially, where the majority of Latino/as live, churches serve as formidable bastions of hope and as catalysts for individual service. Over 47 percent of adult Latino/a Catholics in the Chicago study said that "programs or ministries that help the poor or those in need" was the aspect that "most attracted" them to their parish. Despite this, preliminary findings from our Chicago survey show that Catholic churches in Chicago lag considerably behind Protestants in providing tangible assistance to their members (Table 6).

Though Latino/a Protestant churches outpace their Catholic counterparts in direct assistance to their congregants, Latino/a Catholics in Chicago volunteer outside of their parish at a higher rate than Latino/a Protestants. Nearly 53 percent of Latino/a Catholics volunteer at least once a month for an average of over two hours, compared to 39 percent of Latino/a Protestants. The Chicago survey found that this volunteerism is even stronger among those who have been helped by their congregation. Similarly, in almost every case respondents who said that they had been helped by their congregation were more likely to have helped someone else through a loan or helping find a job.

BELIEFS AND VALUES

Latino/a Catholics—particularly young Latino/a Catholics—are committed to both universal Catholic practices and beliefs and to personal and ethnic expressions of faith. Studies indicate that Latino/as have a somewhat more conservative view of the institutional Church than their non-Hispanic counterparts. Dean Hoge's study of young Catholics found them far more likely to believe that the Catholic Church is the one true Church (64 percent compared to 48 percent of non-Latino/as) and to support orthodox Catholic beliefs such as transubstantiation (Table 7).

Latino/as also highly value their priests, even as they consider the laity important. In the Chicago study, 71 percent of Catholic respondents said there was a good match between their parish and its pastor. And 91 percent of Hoge's young Latino/a Catholics said that lay people are as important to the Church as priests are (Hoge 2001).

On questions of personal and social morality, recent studies have shown that regular religious involvement and attendance have a conservative effect on Catholics and Protestants alike (Pew 2002 National Survey of Latinos; Green et al. 2005). As Table 8 shows, active Latino/a Catholics, defined as those who attend Mass at least once a month, are consistently less accepting of divorce, homosexual relationships, and having a child out of wedlock than inactive Latino/a Catholics. Place of birth also impacts Latino/a beliefs on these matters, with foreign-born Latino/as registering more conservative views than those who were born in the United States.

Preliminary findings from our Chicago survey show marked differences between Latino/a Catholic and Protestant views on these

Table 7. Percent who strongly or moderately agree that:

	Non-Latinos	Latinos
In Mass the bread and wine actually become the body and blood of Christ	87%	95%
The Catholic Church should allow women greater participation in all ministries	87%	87%
Was Jesus Christ God or the Son of God (vs. a prophet, or never lived)?	91%	96%

Source: Young Catholics Survey (Hoge 2001)

Table 8. Moral Issues by Origin and Religious Attendance
Source: 2002 National Survey of Latinos

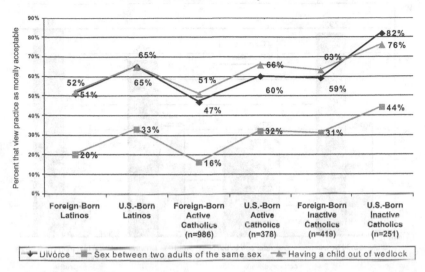

issues. While roughly equal percents of Catholics and Protestants self-identify as religiously conservative, Latino/a Protestants are more likely to believe that the "Bible is the actual Word of God and is to be taken literally, word for word"; that abortion is never permissible; and that the teachings of the Church are unchanging and eternal (Table 9).

CHARISMATIC CHRISTIAN RENEWAL MOVEMENT (CCR) AND LATINO/A FOLK, OR POPULAR, RELIGION

The communal, devotional, and subcultural natures of Latino/a Catholic religious faith are all interwoven with the Charismatic Christian Renewal (CCR) movement. It is difficult to underestimate the impact of this movement upon the religious identity of U.S.-Latino/a Catholics or the influence it has had upon Latino/a Catholic worship-practices. As religion scholar Randall Balmer notes, growing numbers of Latino/a Catholics identify with the CCR (Balmer 2003)

121

Table 9. Religious Values of Chicago Congregants

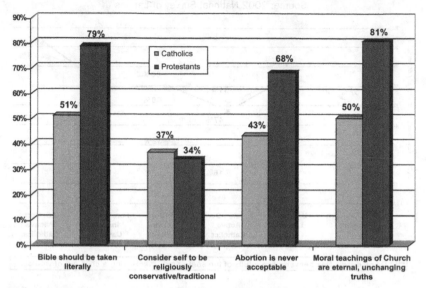

Source: CLCS

and describe themselves by using such language as "the Spirit" and "born-again." The HCAPL study found that more than one-in-four Latino/a Catholics reported having a born-again experience; 86 percent of these are explicitly identified as Pentecostal, Charismatic, or Spirit-filled or as a "Catholic Charismatic" (Table 10).

To date, no comprehensive study has been conducted about the CCR movement and CCR-sympathetic communities. However, observers of these groups note that there can be tension between the CCR Latino/a prayer groups and the parish leadership and hierarchy (USCCB 1999). CCR-sympathetic communities enlist music- and prayer-styles that are very similar to Protestant Pentecostal and Charismatic groups, which can place them at odds with the broader parish's worship-life. This disconnect is furthered by the tendency of these groups to worship in tandem at Sunday afternoon services. But though their individual and communal prayer-lives resemble Evangelical Protestant religious expressions, Gastón Espinosa's ongoing study of Catholic Charismatics has found that they "remain resolutely Catholic in their sensibilities, commitment to the magisterium of the Church, commitment to authority and in their promotion of

Table 10. Percentage of Latino/a Catholics
Who Are Charismatic

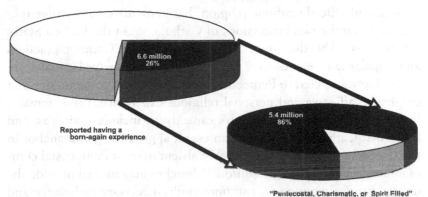

Reported having a
born-again experience

6.6 million
26%

5.4 million
86%

"Pentecostal, Charismatic, or Spirit Filled"
or "Catholic Charismatic"

Source: HCAPL

Catholic spirituality."[20] Espinosa also has observed that Charismatic Latino/a Catholics tend to be more open to allying with conservative Protestants on social and moral issues than non-Charismatics are, since their views on these matters are closer to their Evangelical and Pentecostal Protestant neighbors than to their fellow Catholics.

The tendency of Latino/a Charismatics to identify with both traditional Catholic beliefs and practices and Pentecostal values and worship styles befits the complex nature of Latino/a religiosity. As sociologist Ana María Díaz-Stevens observes, Latino/a religiosity has always been pluralistic, drawing from ancient practices and new revelations and conserving its own traditions while adapting to the pressures of its host cultures (Díaz-Stevens 2003). Its ability to adapt and cross boundaries to create vital and relevant expressions of faith is central. As Díaz-Stevens notes, "Among Hispanics, it is not uncommon to find people simultaneously practicing in different denominations and sometimes even in different religions or combining religious elements that to the outsider may seem incompatible" (Díaz-Stevens 2003).

Though not all expressions of popular religion (Latino/a or otherwise) are consistent with orthodox Catholic theology, the Catholic Church has much to learn from the Latino/a religious experience. But the linguistic and communal isolation that Latino/as often live in from other Catholics is an impediment to this mutual learning experience.

This lack of engagement has helped foster a climate of misunderstanding on both sides. Kenneth Davis, a Franciscan priest and scholar of Latino/a Catholicism, has suggested that the "lack of dialectic between popular and official Catholic religion" has perpetuated a negative tension between the two expressions of Catholicism in the United States (Davis 1994). This disconnect between mainstream Catholic practices and popular faith expressions might be one reason why Latino/as are increasingly attracted to Pentecostal and Evangelical communities that emphasize affective and personal religious experience. Davis remains hopeful of the Catholic Church's capacity to include Latino/as, and notes that Catholicism provides an essential grounding and anchor in the Christian tradition that is notably absent in most Pentecostal communities. He writes, "The traditional churches may indeed provide the unity, historical continuity, and universality necessary to balance and correct popular religion, while Pentecostalism may not" (Davis 1994).

Not all within the Catholic Church share Father Davis's optimism. As the following section addresses, many within the Church are concerned about the seeming defection of Latino/a Catholics to Evangelical and especially Pentecostal expressions of Christianity. Whether CCR functions as a retention mechanism that should be embraced, as a "stepping-stone" to Pentecostal Protestantism, or simply as an example of inculturated Catholicism, is still unclear. Yet it is the very nature of Latino/a Catholicism, with its history of adapting indigenous and folk religious practices, that provides both the possibility of defection and the renewal of the Catholic Church. Latino/as have survived and thrived, and in many ways are renewing the Church in the United States through their active engagement and vibrant religious identity.

Latino/as Moving Away from Catholicism

In 1988, sociologist and priest Andrew Greeley lifted a call of alarm at the growing number of Latino/a Catholics who were leaving the Church. Terming it the "worst defection in the history of the Catholic Church in the United States" (Greeley 1988), he later proclaimed his astonishment at how little response his earlier warning engendered (Greeley 1997). While Greeley's predictions concerning Latino/a conversion to mainline Protestantism and his claim that Protestantism facilitates upward status mobility for Latino/as have been disputed (Hunt 1998, Hernández 1999), his general theories concerning both the institutional characteristics of religious denominations and the social aspects of religion still dominate. The concern of this section is to explore the trends in religious "switching." Are Latino/a Catholics becoming Evangelical or Pentecostal Protestants? If so, to what extent, and what characterizes those who switch? Why are they switching? How can or should the U.S. Catholic Church respond?[21]

LEAVING THE CHURCH

Greeley's alarm about the trend toward Protestantism was certainly justified. While immigration has increased the number of Latino/as in both the general population and the Catholic Church over the last thirty years, the number of Latino/as who self-identify as Protestant or even non-religious continues to rise.

In the HCAPL study, Gastón Espinosa and his colleagues found that, while the overall percentage of Latino/as who identify as Catholics continues to hover around 70 percent, this is mainly due to the high proportion of Mexican immigrants who are Catholic.[22] Most (23 percent) of the remaining 30 percent in the HCAPL study identified as Protestant, and 85 percent of these described themselves as born-again or Evangelical (Espinosa et al. 2003).

When the level of inculturation, measured by the number of generations someone and their family have lived in the United States, is taken into account, the shifts become significantly more dramatic. Only 62 percent of U.S.-born Latino/as in the HCAPL study identified as Catholic, and other polls have found even more dramatic shifts between first- and second-generation Latino/as (Perl et al. 2004).

A further analysis of these trends in Hernández (2006) compares the 1999 National Survey on Latino/as in America with the 2002 and 2004 Pew National Surveys of Latinos. In this study, Hernández found sharper shifts in the decline of Catholics especially among third-generation Latino/as and a corresponding increase in the proportion of

Table 11. Latino/a Religious Change Across Generations (1999–2004)

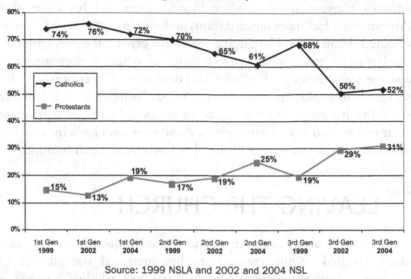

Source: 1999 NSLA and 2002 and 2004 NSL

Protestants in each generation. As Table 11 shows, Latino/as are becoming more Protestant the longer they are in the United States.

WHO'S LEAVING AND WHY

Converting to a different religion is a dramatic process that potentially alters the way people think, act, and live. This process of conversion is facilitated by both institutional and social incentives. American pluralism offers the opportunity for religious "competition" not found in many other contexts, giving Latino/as and other religious "consumers" many religious groups from which to choose.

Though religious switching occurs in all religious communities, some scholars have suggested that Catholicism may be uniquely susceptible. Allan Figueroa Deck points out that the structure of the Catholic Church may challenge its ability to relate to popular indigenous forms of religious practice or to make the necessary adaptations for its Spanish-speaking members (Deck 1992). The lack of Latino clergy exacerbates the cultural dilemma, and the indigenous leadership and cultural relevancy found in many Latino/a Evangelical/Pentecostal communities adds to their appeal.

The comparatively small size of Protestant communities encourages a more intense level of identification and involvement within these religious congregations. Among our Chicago adults, Protestants were more than twice as likely to spend two or more hours a week at church, to tithe over $50 a month, and to give a "high" proportion of their income to the church (Table 12). The more negative view that Evangelical and Pentecostal communities express toward the "world" further engenders a strong sense of community and attachment within the congregation.

One explanation for why Latino/as join Protestant churches posits that this switching is a function of acculturation and integration within larger American society, and that a desire to assimilate lies behind much of the conversion rates (Hurtado 1995; Stevens-Arroyo and Díaz Arroyo 1998; Marín and Gamba 1993). This is closely linked to the culture-denying hypothesis that cites the desire to abandon one's cultural identity and traditions as an explanatory factor in conversion. But though there is some evidence of a higher rate of conversion among Latino/as from the middle classes, from English speakers, and from third- or more generation residents (Hunt 1998, Greeley 1988), the preliminary CSLC data confound this theory. Adults in Chicago who had converted from Catholicism to Protestantism did have better English skills, but did not have significantly different income or education levels from their Catholic counterparts (Hernández 1999).

These findings are consistent with Hunt's 1998 analysis of the 1984 National Alcohol Survey, in which he finds little indication that Protestantism is associated with upward social mobility among Latino/as. Thus contrary to the culture-denying hypothesis, Evangelical and Pentecostal "storefront" congregations may in fact help redefine the cultural identity of their members' originating countries in

Table 12. Involvement Level with Congregation

	Catholics	Protestants
Spend more than two hours a week at church	24%	62%
Tithe more than $50 a month	28%	70%
Tithe a "high" proportion of income	20%	44%

Source: CLCS

Table 13. Which aspects of your congregation life most attract you?

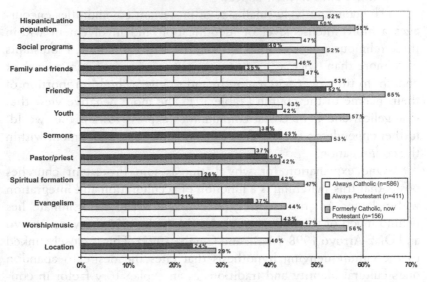

Hispanic/Latino population
- 52%
- 50%
- 58%

Social programs
- 47%
- 40%
- 52%

Family and friends
- 46%
- 35%
- 47%

Friendly
- 53%
- 52%
- 65%

Youth
- 43%
- 42%
- 57%

Sermons
- 38%
- 43%
- 53%

Pastor/priest
- 37%
- 40%
- 42%

Spiritual formation
- 26%
- 42%
- 47%

Evangelism
- 21%
- 37%
- 44%

Worship/music
- 43%
- 47%
- 56%

Location
- 40%
- 24%
- 29%

Legend:
- □ Always Catholic (n=586)
- ■ Always Protestant (n=411)
- ▨ Formerly Catholic, now Protestant (n=156)

Source: CLCS

a way that is adaptable to the new environment (Hernández 1999). The independent and highly localized nature of these communities, along with their small sizes, allows congregants to participate in shaping the cultural and religious identity of the church—something that is harder to do within the organizational structure of the Catholic parish.

Social influences and relationships are also key in the conversion process. Despite the cultural tensions, and the difficulty that Latino/as can have finding a place in the U.S. Catholic Church, they are not likely to convert unless there are other people they know and trust who are affiliated with Protestant denominations. A 1994 survey of current Latino/a Seventh-day Adventists found that 73 percent of former Catholics said that their "very first contact with the Seventh-day Adventist Church" was through a friend or a relative. But though friends and relatives often serve as a gateway to Protestant communities, those who become active soon take on the theological and spiritual views of their adopted churches. Thus, when the same former Latino/a Catholic Adventists who had initially attended their congregation because of relationships were asked about the "main reason that most attracted" them to the Adventist message, only 37 percent still said family, a close friend, or the warmth and caring of the congregation, while 69 percent offered theological explanations such as "truth of message" or the "plan of salvation."

Participants in our Chicago survey who had converted to Protestantism overwhelmingly emphasized the relational aspects of their adopted congregations. When asked about the most attractive qualities of their church/parish, 65 percent of former Catholics members of Protestant churches in Chicago said its "friendliness," and 47 percent the "presence of family and friends." Other responses from Chicago adults shed light on the relationship between Catholics, former Catholics, and Protestants (Table 13).

Not surprisingly, the converts in our study are almost universally more enthusiastic about their congregations than either their lifelong-Catholic or cradle-Protestant counterparts. In general, former Catholics share active Catholics' appreciation for the social aspects of their congregations, and value the same "theological" characteristics of their churches as their more recent Protestant kin. Both Catholics (46 percent) and former Catholics (47 percent) say they appreciate their church because "their family and friends attend here," and both highly value their churches' social programs (Catholics—47 percent; former

Table 14. Worship Attendance of Chicago Congregants

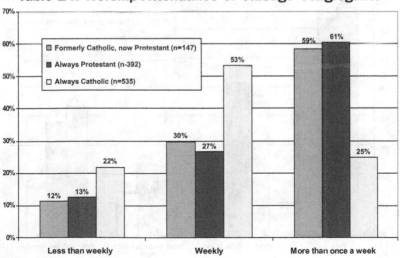

Source: CLCS

Catholics—52 percent). Conversely, former Catholics are more like lifelong Protestants in valuing the evangelism, spiritual formation, and sermons of their congregations.

Former Catholics also have taken on the behaviors and values of their new communities, with higher worship-attendance patterns than Catholics (Table 14, p. 129). Their religious practices reflect and often surpass the trends within the Latino/a Protestant community as well. Like lifelong Protestants, they are more apt than Catholics to engage in the devotional activities shown in Table 15, but they are *more* likely than cradle Protestants to pray individually and with their families on a daily basis (Table 15).

Similarly, former Catholics are more like Protestants regarding religious values. While roughly one-third of all three groups consider themselves religiously conservative/traditional, Protestants and former Catholics are far more likely to take the Bible literally, to believe that abortion is never acceptable, and to say that the moral teachings of the Church are eternal and unchanging (Table 16).

But though former Catholics and cradle Protestants hold more conservative religious views than Catholics, significantly *higher* percents of both Protestant groups believe that women should be allowed

Table 15. Religious Practices of Latino/as

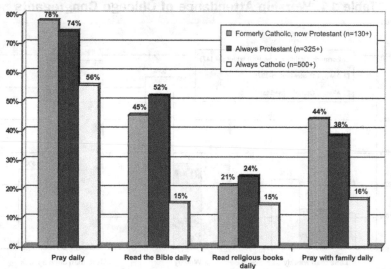

Legend:
- ▨ Formerly Catholic, now Protestant (n=130+)
- ■ Always Protestant (n=325+)
- ☐ Always Catholic (n=500+)

Practice	Formerly Catholic, now Protestant	Always Protestant	Always Catholic
Pray daily	78%	74%	56%
Read the Bible daily	45%	52%	15%
Read religious books daily	21%	24%	15%
Pray with family daily	44%	38%	16%

Source: CLCS

to be pastors or priests than their Catholic counterparts (Table 17). Converts to Protestantism fall almost directly between the two other groups on this issue, and are notably less supportive of women ministers than lifelong Protestants are. While the data does not show whether the role of women was a reason for converting to Protestantism, this finding does indicate an interesting difference in views toward religious authority and leadership.

For many Latino/as the disruptions of immigration and cultural tension also bring the opportunity to forge new identities. While individuals may have defined themselves as Catholic in one context, new situations such as geographic relocations, increased education, exogamous marriage, and reduced contact with relatives open opportunities for new religious preference (Sherkat and Wilson 1995, Loveland 2001). Many of the trends explored above are part of this process.

How to Respond

The Catholic Church in the United States has often been described as a "wide tent" under which regional and cultural variances are unified by core beliefs and practices. Though tensions certainly

Table 16. Religious Values of Latino/as

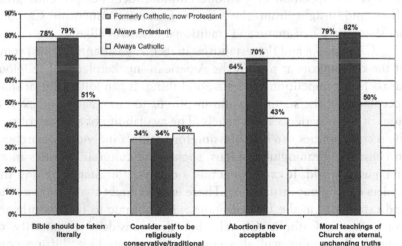

Source: CLCS

Table 17. Percentage Agreeing That Women Should Be Allowed to Be Pastors/Priests

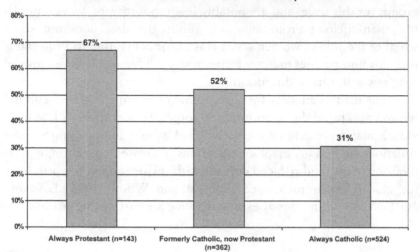

Source: CLCS

have arisen around what constitutes continuity of faith and what are acceptable reinterpretations, the Church's history of welcoming and incorporating the practices and traditions of newcomers can serve as a strong foundation from which to face the challenge of including Latino/as more fully. However, forging a unified community to embrace the spectrum of Catholic Latino/a identities portends great effort and insight from the clergy, European American Catholic parishes, and Charismatic and traditional Latino/as alike.

Catholicism and Protestantism, in its many variants, are just some of the competitors at play in the American "marketplace" of religious ideas. This competition can be a good thing. It can jolt us out of staid acceptance of the status quo and inspire us to more authentic expressions of our experiences and beliefs. The availability of an array of religious communities can be a blessing for Latino/a individuals searching to construct meaningful religious, social, and cultural identities in an ambiguous world. It can also act as a catalyst for change among the leaders of religious institutions. There is little doubt that Latino/a faith and experience in the United States will continue to find its primary home in the Catholic Church. But the considerable minority of Latino/a Protestants will also continue to grow. This shifting constituency and the dynamics of conversionary religion, as Díaz-Stevens asserts, "will push the Roman Catholic Church once again towards 'innovative' approaches and...serve to invigorate Christianity and religion in contemporary U.S. Society" (Díaz-Stevens 1998).

It is difficult to ascertain if the behavior and belief trends and differences of former Catholics described above are the result of their residence within Protestant congregations, of their reflections upon Latino/a life in the United States, or of authentic values that are unaddressed by the U.S. Catholic institution. Despite the last, there are specific ways in which the Catholic Church can take action to reach out to Latino/as, particularly in the areas of social justice, youth, leadership, and worship-life.

SOCIAL JUSTICE

Although social justice and a concern for inequality has been a foundational aspect of the Catholic Church, a majority of Catholics do not identify the Church's social teachings as pivotal to Catholic identity. A survey conducted in 1999 found that 56 percent of Catholics believe that someone can be a good Catholic without donating time or money to help the poor (D'Antonio et al. 2001). William D'Antonio and his colleagues suggest that while Catholics affirm the Church's social teachings, actual concrete action "seems more like an option than an expectation of a responsible Catholic" (D'Antonio et al. 2001).

The Church could better mobilize its other members to reach out to their Latino/a brothers and sisters by placing a greater emphasis on the Church's social teachings, and by reminding European American Catholics of the Church's history of outreach to previous waves of immigrants. Latino/as value the social justice tradition of the Catholic Church and need its advocacy. Yet Protestant congregations seem to be more effective at organizing and delivering services to their immediate members than Catholic parishes. While large-parish structures may be a barrier to service provision, the U.S. Catholic Church must continue to seek ways to build a stronger sense of community at the local church level that encourages parishioners to respond to each other's physical and spiritual needs.

YOUTH

Among the congregational characteristics that we asked the Chicago survey participants to evaluate, 57 percent of former Catholics were attracted to their adopted congregations' attention to youth. In comparison, only 43 percent of Catholics praised their parishes' youth programming. Latino/a youth are the fastest-growing demographic of the U.S. Catholic Church. The same recommendations that Dean Hoge cites for the Church regarding young Catholics in general are relevant to its strategy to reach Latino/as as well (Hoge 2001):

- Be more welcoming to young adults by listening to their concerns.
- Provide ways in which young adults can become meaningfully involved.
- Provide more adult education, and more study of scripture and the faith.
- Address the disparity between Church teachings and the realities of sexuality of young adults.

The Church must take seriously the discipleship of the young generation, creating pathways of learning and assimilation into the life of the Church. In a tradition that tends to favor age and authority, the questions and concerns of youth must be given a central place or they will look elsewhere for answers.

LEADERSHIP

While the current clergy needs continued equipping for ministry in the Latino/a context, recruitment of Latino/as to the future clergy, especially those born in the United States, must be a priority. The recruitment of Latino/as to the priesthood and lay ecclesial leadership is directly related to the recommendations about increasing the Church's youth ministries. Recognition of multiple expressions of congregational life, fostering alternative pathways to leadership, and continued development of authentic indigenous religious culture among Latino/as will create the context for new leadership to emerge.

The role of the laity must also be recognized more fully by the institutional leadership. Developing training-models and resources for lay Latino/a leadership promises great dividends for future leadership and community.

WORSHIP LIFE

If we are correct in asserting that religious practice is a means to redefining cultural identity, the Church must create an environment that allows Latino/as to *be* the Church. Unlike past immigrant groups who brought their clergy and structures to a relatively open landscape, Latino/as in the United States bring little more than the passion of their faith to a firmly established institution. Latino/as are already changing the face of Catholic worship-practice through the incorporation of its musical styles, Spanish language, and devotional practices. While cultural and language barriers can impede greater incorporation, the way ahead requires deliberate engagement and a commitment to respect the religious experiences and expressions of Latino/as.

The Catholic Church in the United States and abroad can expect further competition. As the Latino/a presence continues to grow in this country, other religious communities will respond to their spiritual, social, and physical needs through innovative ministries and adaptive worship. But the Catholic Church has the advantages of incumbency and cultural continuity upon which it may build. Its success may be predicated upon its willingness to adapt and be changed.

NOTES

1. Latino and Hispanic are both language constructs of the United States that refer to peoples who share linguistic, geographic, and cultural traditions. In fact, many Latino/as in the United States primarily think of themselves by country of origin, e.g., Mexican, Puerto Rican, Guatemalan, or simply as American. In this paper we have cho-

sen to use Latino because of its distinctiveness apart from the Spanish colonial culture and the word *Latino/a* because of its gender inclusivity.

2. Based on the U.S. Census Bureau's population estimates of July 1, 2005: Hispanics (14.4%), Black alone 37.9 million (12.8%), Asian alone 12.5 million (4.2%).

3. The Pew Hispanic Center reports that 9.2 percent of Hispanic women had a birth in the past year, White alone 6.3 percent, Black alone 7.4 percent, Asian alone 7 percent (Pew Hispanic Center 2006). The 1996 fertilization rate for the general population was 2.03, and 3.0 for Hispanics (McFalls 1998).

4. U.S. Census data for 2004 reports that 34 percent of Latino/as are under the age of eighteen, compared to 24 percent of non-Hispanic whites.

5. According to the Pew Hispanic Center, the average family income in 2003 for unauthorized migrants who had lived in the country for less than ten years was $25,700, while those who had been in the country for a decade or more earned $29,900. In contrast, average family incomes were considerably higher for both legal immigrants ($47,800) and native-born Latino/as ($47,700) (Passel 2005).

6. Seventy percent is an estimate based on a review of literature performed by Paul Perl, Jennifer Greely, and Mark Gray, which is available at the Web site of the Center for Applied Research in the Apostolate (CARA) (http://cara.georgetown.edu).

7. For more information on the 2004 and 2002 national surveys of Latinos, visit the Pew Hispanic Center's website: www.pewhispanic. org.

8. Total population of U.S. Hispanics: U.S. Census Bureau, Census Brief, May 2001.

9. Survey commissioned by the Latino Coalition and conducted by McLaughlin and Associates' Opiniones Latinas, Washington, DC, August 2002.

10. Compiled by Instituto Fe y Vida research services: http://feyvida.org/research/fastfacts.html.

11. Ibid.

12. USCCB Committee on Hispanic Affairs, 1999. "Hispanic Ministry at the Turn of the New Millennium," p. 5. Study conducted by Stewart Lawrence of Puentes, Inc.

13. Instituto Fe y Vida.

14. Ibid.

15. USCCB Secretariat for Hispanic Affairs. The National Association of Hispanic Priests reported 2,900 Latino priests, and approximately 46,000 priests in the United States were reported in the 2002 Official Catholic Directory.

16. Instituto Fe y Vida.

17. United States Conference of Catholic Bishops.

18. Ibid.

19. The CLCS methodology employed a random sampling of one hundred churches stratified by religious denominations (oversampling for smaller denominations) in the Chicago area with a majority Latino/a attendance (n=606). After an initial survey of clergy from the population, the second phase consisted of face-to-face interviews with clergy of the congregations in the sample. Most of the statistics reported in this paper are from surveys completed by adults among this one-hundred-church sample.

20. From e-mail correspondence with Gastón Espinosa (August 5, 2006), based upon his ongoing study of Latino/a Pentecostals and Charismatics.

21. As articulated earlier, this paper does not seek to assess directly the role of the Catholic Charismatic Renewal movement either in Latino/a religious switching or as an alternative to official Catholicism, but its significance must not be underestimated. For further information see Manuel Vásquez, "Charismatic Renewal among Latino Catholics," in *Religions of the United States in Practice*, vol. 2, ed. Colleen McDannell (Princeton: Princeton University Press, 2000).

22. Although Latino/a immigration to the United States is overwhelmingly Mexican, and Mexicans are overwhelmingly Catholic, recent research shows that approximately 12.4 percent of all Mexican immigrants to the United States are now Protestant (Jasso et al. 2002).

REFERENCES

Andrade, Juan, Andrew Hernández, and Laura Barberena-Medrano. 2002. *The Almanac of Latino/a Politics 2002–2004*. Chicago, IL: The United States Hispanic Leadership Institute.

Archdiocese of Chicago. 2005. "Data Composite: Facts and Figures for Year Ending 2004." From www.archdiocese-chgo.org.

Balmer, Randall. 2003. "Crossing the Borders: Evangelicalism and Migration." In Yvonne Yazbeck Haddad, Jane I. Smith, and John L. Esposito, eds., *Religion and Immigration: Christian, Jewish, and Muslim Experiences in the United States*, 53–60. Walnut Creek, CA: AltaMira Press.

Cadena, Gilbert R. 1995. "Religious Ethnic Identity: A Socio-Religious Portrait of Latinas and Latinos in the Catholic Church." In Anthony M. Stevens-Arroyo and Gilbert R. Cadena, eds., *Old Masks, New Faces: Religion and Latino/a Identities*. New York: Bildner Center for Western Hemisphere Studies.

D'Antonio, William V., James. D. Davidson, Dean R. Hoge, and Katherine Meyer. 2001. *American Catholics: Gender, Generation and Commitment*. Walnut Creek, CA: AltaMira Press.

Davis, Kenneth G. 1994. "Brevia from the Hispanic Shift: Continuity Rather than Conversion?" In Anthony M. Stevens-Arroyo and Ana María Díaz-Stevens, eds., *An Enduring Flame: Studies on Latino/a Popular Religiosity*. New York: Bildner Center for Western Hemisphere Studies.

Davis, Kenneth G. 1994. "The Hispanic Shift: Continuity Rather than Conversion?" *Journal of Hispanic/Latino/a Theology* 1/3 (1994): 68.

Davis, Kenneth G., Andrew Hernández, and Philip E. Lampe. 2005. "Summary of Hispanic Catholic Leadership: Key to the Future." In Edwin I. Hernández, Milagros Peña, Kenneth Davis, and Elizabeth Station, eds., *Strengthening Hispanic Ministry Across Denominations: A Call to Action*. Durham, NC: Duke Divinity School.

Deck, Allan Figueroa. 1998. "Latino Leaders for Church and Society: Critical Issues." In Peter Casarella and Raúl Gómez, eds., *El Cuerpo de Cristo: The Hispanic Presence in the U.S. Catholic Church*. New York: Crossroad Publishing.

Díaz-Stevens, Ana María. 1998. "The Hispanic Challenge to U.S. Catholicism: Colonialism, Migration, and Religious Adaptation." In Peter Casarella and Raúl Gómez, eds., *El Cuerpo de Cristo: The Hispanic Presence in the U.S. Catholic Church*. New York: Crossroad Publishing.

Díaz-Stevens, Ana María. 2003. "Colonization versus Immigration in the Integration and Identification of Hispanics in the United States." In Yvonne Yazbeck Haddad, Jane I. Smith, and John L.

Esposito, eds., *Religion and Immigration: Christian, Jewish, and Muslim Experiences in the United States.* Walnut Creek, CA: AltaMira Press.

Espinosa, Gastón, Virgilio Elizondo, and Jesse Miranda. 2003. "Hispanic Churches in American Public Life: Summary of Findings." Interim Report, 2003, vol. 2 (January), Institute of Latino Studies, University of Notre Dame.

Froehle, Bryan T., and Mary L. Gautier. 2000. *Catholicism USA: A Portrait of the Catholic Church in the United States.* Maryknoll, NY: Orbis Press.

Gray, Mark M., and Mary L. Gautier. 2005. "Summary of Latino/a Catholic Leaders in the United States." In Edwin I. Hernández, Milagros Peña, Kenneth Davis, and Elizabeth Station, eds., *Strengthening Hispanic Ministry Across Denominations: A Call to Action.* Durham, NC: Duke Divinity School.

Greeley, Andrew. 1988. "Defection among Hispanics." *America* 30: 61–62.

Greeley, Andrew. 1997. "Defection among Hispanics (Updated)." *America* 177(8): 12–14.

Green, John C., Corwin E. Smidt, James L. Guth, and Lyman A. Kellstedt. 2005. "The American Religious Landscape and the 2004 Presidential Vote." Washington, DC: The Pew Forum on Religion & Public Life.

Hernández, Edwin I. 1999. "Moving from the Cathedral to Storefront Churches: Understanding Religious Growth and Decline Among Latino/a Protestants." In David Maldonado, Jr., ed., *Protestantes/Protestants: Hispanic Christianity with Mainline Traditions.* Nashville, TN: Abingdon Press.

Hernández, Edwin I., Kenneth G. Davis, Milagros Peña, Georgian Schiopu, and Jeffrey Smith. 2005. "Latina/o Religious Realignment and the Changing Moral Landscape of Life in the U.S." Paper presented at the Changing Face of American Evangelism conference by the Institute for the Study of American Evangelicals, Wheaton College, Wheaton, Il, 2005. Timothy Tseng and Michael O. Emerson, eds., *The Changing Face of American Evangelism* (collection of conference papers, forthcoming).

Hoge, Dean R. 2001. *Young Adult Catholics.* Notre Dame, IN: University of Notre Dame Press.

Hoge, Dean R. 2002. *The First Five Years of the Priesthood.* Collegeville, MN: The Liturgical Press.

Hunt, Larry L. 1998. "The Spirit of Hispanic Protestantism in the United States: National Survey Comparisons of Catholics and Non-Catholics." *Social Science Quarterly* 79:828–45.

Hurtado, Aida. 1995. "Variations, Combinations, and Evolutions: Latino Families in the United States." In *Understanding Latino Families: Scholarship, Policy and Practice.* Ed. Ruth Zambrana. Thousand Oaks, CA: Sage Publications Press.

Instituto Fe y Vida. Found on April 17, 2006, at http://feyvida.org/research/fastfacts.html.

Jasso, Guillermina, Douglas S. Massey, Mark R. Rosenzweig, and James P. Smith. 2003. "Exploring the Religious Preference of Recent Immigrants to the United States: Evidence from the New Immigrant Survey Pilot." In Yvonne Yazbeck Haddad, Jane I. Smith, and John L. Esposito, eds., *Religion and Immigration: Christian, Jewish, and Muslim Experiences in the United States.* Walnut Creek, CA: AltaMira Press.

John Paul II. 1999. "Ecclesia in America." Downloaded on May 14, 2006, from http://www.vatican.va/holy_father/john_paul_ii/apost_exhortations/documents/hf_jp-ii_exh_22011999_ecclesia-in-america_en.html.

Loveland, Matthew. 2003. "Religious Switching: Preference Development, Maintenance, and Change." *Journal for the Scientific Study of Religion* 42:1 (2003): 147–57.

Marin, Gerardo, and Raymond Gamba. 1993. "The Role of Expectations in Religious Conversations: The Case of Hispanic Catholics." *Review of Religious Research* 34:357–71.

Passel, Jeffrey S. 2005. *Unauthorized Migrants: Numbers and Characteristics.* Washington, DC: Pew Hispanic Center.

Passel, Jeffrey S. and Roberto Suro. 2005. *Rise, Peak, and Decline: Trends in U.S. Immigration 1992–2004.* Washington, DC: Pew Hispanic Center.

Peña, Milagros, and Lisa Frehill. 1998. "Latina Religious Practice: Analyzing Cultural Dimensions in measures of Religiosity." *Journal for the Scientific Study of Religion* 37(4):620–35.

Perl, Paul, Jennifer Z. Greely, and Mark M. Gray. 2004. Paper presented at the 2004 meeting of the Association for the Sociology of Religion and accessible on the Web site of Center for Applied Research in the Apostolate. http://cara.georgetown.edu.

Pew Hispanic Center. 2005. *Hispanics: A People in Motion*. Washington, DC.

Pew Hispanic Center. 2006. *A Statistical Portrait of Hispanics at Mid-Decade*. At http://pewhispanic.org/reports/middecade/.

Ramirez, Roberto R., and Patricia de la Cruz. 2002. "The Hispanic Population in the United States: March 2002," Current Population Reports, P20–545. Washington, DC: U.S. Census Bureau.

Rosado, Caleb. 1995. "The Concept of 'Pueblo' as a Paradigm for Explaining the Religious Experience of Latino/as." In Anthony M. Stevens-Arroyo and Gilbert R. Cadena, eds., *Old Masks, New Faces: Religion and Latino/a Identities*. New York: Bildner Center for Western Hemisphere Studies.

Sherkat, Darren, and John Wilson. 1995. "Preferences, Constraints, and Choices in Religious Markets: An Examination of Religious Switching and Apostasy." *Social Forces* 73:933–1026.

Stevens-Arroyo, Anthony, and Ana Maria Diaz-Stevens. 1998. *Recognizing the Latino/a Resurgence in U.S. Religion: The Emmas Paradigm*. Colorado, CO: Westview Press.

Stoops, Nicole. 2004. "Educational Attainment in the United States: 2003." Washington, DC: U.S. Census Bureau.

Suro, Roberto, and Audrey Singer. 2002. "Latino/a Growth in Metropolitan America: Changing Patterns, New Locations." Washington, DC: Pew Hispanic Center.

U.S. Census Bureau. 2001. "The Hispanic Population in the United States: Population Characteristics." March 2001.

U.S. Census Bureau. 2004. "Income, Poverty, and Health Insurance Coverage in the United States: 2004."

USCCB. 1999. "Hispanic Ministry at the Turn of the New Millennium: A Report of the Bishops' Committee on Hispanic Affairs." Online only. http://www.nccbuscc.org/hispanicaffairs/study.shtml.

Vásquez, Manuel. 2000. "Charismatic Renewal among Latino Catholics." In Colleen McDannell, ed., *Religions of the United States in Practice*, vol. 2. Princeton, NJ: Princeton University Press.

Wuthnow, Robert. 2000. Religion and Politics Survey. Princeton, NJ: University Survey Research Center.

Trends in Global Christianity

Implications for the New Evangelization

Philip Jenkins

St. Vincent de Paul (1580–1660) was a great Catholic saint and, in his own way, a prophetic voice in the Church. The 1640s was one of the bloodiest decades in European history, a time in which Catholics were killing Protestants, Protestants were killing Catholics, Christians were killing Jews, and everyone was killing anyone suspected of being a witch. At the time, St. Vincent de Paul made an interesting comment: "Jesus said his Church would last until the end of time," he noted. "But he never mentioned Europe." The Church of the future, he said as far back as 1640, would be the Church of South America, Africa, China, and Japan. Although we might argue about the inclusion of Japan in that list, we should recall that twentieth-century Japan was home to Shusaku Endo (1923–1996), one of the greatest Catholic novelists of the last century. However, the point I wish to make is quite simple: Christianity, a religion that was born in Africa and Asia, has now decided to go home. Our traditional concept of the Christian world as a predominantly white and Euro-American world is no longer the norm. It has been replaced by Nigerian villagers worshipping in a small, rural village church and by Brazilians living in the *favelas* of Rio de Janeiro worshipping around a makeshift altar. Perhaps John

142

Updike's observation that "God sticks pretty close to the equator" is indeed true!

In the world today, there are around about 2.1 billion Christians. Of those, about 531 million live in Europe. The second largest contingent lives in Latin America, where there are about 511 million Christians. The third largest group is in Africa with about 389 million members, followed by Asia with 344 million Christians. Some 226 million Christian believers live in North America.[1]

These figures change rapidly, however, when you project them into the future. By 2025, Africa and Latin America will be competing for the title of "Most Christian Continent of the World." In the long run, Africa will win. By 2050, Christianity will be the religion of Africa and the African diaspora. By then, there will be about three billion Christians in the world. Of those, the proportion of those who will be white and who will not be Latino will be only somewhere between one-fifth and one-sixth of the total. Looking at projections for the year 2050 regarding the Christian population of the world, the United States will be at the head of the list of individual countries, followed by such countries as Brazil, Mexico, the Philippines, Nigeria, the Congo, Ethiopia, and China. However, many of the Christians in the United States at that time will be of Hispanic, Asian, or African origin. In fact, by the year 2050, one-third of all Americans will have Latino or Asian roots—roots that will be overwhelmingly Christian. This does not include those Americans of African origin, people who are either African Americans or of more recent African stock. In a sense, the notion of "Western Christianity" that we still speak of today will be a memory of the past.[2]

When you look at figures like this, there is always a temptation to quote them at length because so many of them demand to be quoted. So let me give you some additional figures. First of all, let us look at Christianity in Africa during the twentieth century. In 1900, Africa had 10 million Christians representing about 10 percent of the population. By the year 2000, this figure had grown to 360 million, representing about half of the population. Quantitatively, this is the *largest* shift in religious affiliation that has ever occurred. Focusing on the demographic change in the Catholic population alone, Africa had 1.9 million Catholics in 1900. By 2000, the Catholic population of the continent had risen to 130 million, representing a gross increase of *6,708 percent!*[3]

Yet another figure for the Catholic world should give us pause. There were more Catholic baptisms last year in the Philippines than in France, Spain, Italy, and Poland combined.[4] Indeed, the Philippines are a prime example of a Catholic society that has maintained its Catholic loyalty to this day, especially in face of the growing Pentecostal tide. Anywhere you go in the United States or Europe today, you will find Filipinos practicing their faith. When you read about Filipinos who are being flogged or executed in the non-Christian world for practicing their faith, they generally belong to one of the great transnational, Charismatic religious groups that originated in the Philippines such as El Shaddai and Bukas Loob sa Diyos—Catholic organizations that deserve our interest, respect, and research.

Where are Catholics in the world today? Many names are familiar: Brazil, Mexico, the United States, the countries of Latin America, and the Philippines. The nations of Europe—Italy, France, Spain, and Poland—still figure in the list. These countries currently form the top ten. But the demographics will change within the next twenty to twenty-five years. As we all know, children are central to the growth of any religion or religious organization, but the situation changes when a society's birthrate dips and there are very few children. In a worst case scenario, the Church will eventually decline and die out in these places. This is what is happening in Europe, for example. In the past, priests in these countries were preparing one hundred children for confirmation at a time; today they are preparing only three or four. This is another reason why the Catholic world will be shifting globally to the South.

As I pointed out earlier, there were 130 million Catholics in Africa as of the year 2000—approximately one-eighth of the world's Catholics. This figure is projected to rise to 230 million by the year 2025, and African Catholics will then represent one-sixth of all members of the Catholic Church worldwide.[5] By 2025, approximately 60 percent of Catholics around the world will probably live in Africa and Latin America alone—not counting the Philippines, China, or India—and the number should reach two-thirds before 2050. At that point, European and Euro-American Catholics will be a small fragment of a church dominated by Filipinos, Mexicans, Vietnamese, and Congolese. "From 2004 to 2050, Catholic populations are projected to increase by 146 percent in Africa, 63 percent in Asia, 42 percent in Latin America and the Caribbean, and 38 percent in North America," sociologist

Rogelio Saenz affirms. "Meanwhile, Europe will experience a 6 percent decline in its Catholic population between 2004 and 2050."[6]

When you consider Africa, Asia, and Latin America as a whole, the countries of these parts of the world currently account for two-thirds of all Catholics worldwide. However, this figure does not include people of Global South stock who are living in the Global North, such as Latino Catholics in the United States. By 2025, 75 percent of U.S. Catholics will trace their origins to Africa, Asia, and Latin America, and the figure will continue to grow throughout the century. If you include the people of Latino origin who live in the Global North—including the 50 million or so people in the United States who will probably be of Mexican descent by the year 2050—approximately 80 percent of the Roman Catholic Church will be comprised of individuals who live in or trace their origins to the Global South by the middle of the century.[7]

Here is one additional figure on which to reflect: 2.36 percent. Let me explain. This is the rate of Christian growth in Africa *per year*. This means that the number of Christians in Africa will double in thirty years or so. Although there are many reasons for the Muslim-Christian tensions that exist in many parts of Africa such as Nigeria, the principal reason can be attributed to the fact that Muslims are terrified that their children will eventually become Christian. Back in the year 1900, in the lands that make up the country of Nigeria, 1 percent of the people were Christian and 33 percent were Muslim. In other words, Muslims outnumbered Christians by 33 to 1. By 1970, the two religions had reached parity at 45 percent each. Today, if you look at internal surveys (which no one will publish for fear of creating religious unrest), the slim majority of the population in Nigeria is Christian.[8]

If Christianity were simply moving south in the sense of merely becoming a religion increasingly characterized by people of different ethnic backgrounds, that in itself would be interesting. But something more noteworthy is occurring. As Christianity moves south into different cultures, it has been acquiring a cultural aspect from each of the societies with which it has contact. Much of what we in the Global North consider Christianity is, in fact, Western Christianity. It is a Euro-American Christianity. With the shift in demographics, however, we have to learn to look at Christian history in a different light. We have to rid ourselves of the idea of Christianity as moving from

Palestine, expanding across the Mediterranean into Europe, and then reaching a happy climax by crossing the Atlantic to America. Indeed, Christianity did move north at first, but at the same time it was also moving east and south. By the time Christianity reached Anglo-Saxon England in the seventh century, there were Christians in Ethiopia who were in their *tenth* generation. Likewise, by the time Christian missionaries reached Anglo-Saxon London, other missionaries were reaching the capital of China. Around the year 1000, there were considerably more Christians in Asia than in Europe. When Christian missionaries reached Africa in the nineteenth century, they were often puzzled as to the grand reception they received. Their popularity was due to the fact that they were bringing back the "old" religion. This is a whole history that our modern age has often overlooked and forgotten.

If you look at the character of the Christianity that is growing so rapidly in the Global South, in some ways it looks strange and bizarre to us Christians in the West. But in many ways, it has an ancient, authentic feel that is rather difficult for us to recapture. Whole portions of scripture, for example, that we approach out of archaeological interest come alive for people from Global-South societies. For example, the Book of Ruth is immensely popular in Africa and much of Asia because it is essentially the story about a society destroyed by a famine that breaks up families. The men are able to escape, but women have to remain behind with the children and they struggle to maintain the integrity of their society. The Book of Ruth communicates some important lessons regarding family obligations and obligations to our kin. It contains some lessons for modern society about our responsibilities to the fellow members of our church or parish, such as finding them jobs and putting food on their tables.

Likewise, the Epistle of James is also immensely popular in Africa. The Epistle of James has had a controversial history in the West. In the Protestant tradition, Martin Luther was not sure that it should be included in the New Testament. He thought it was a little too Catholic on the subject of works versus faith. Yet, there is one verse that has consistently been the subject of sermons in churches in West Africa: "You have no idea what your life will be like tomorrow. You are a puff of smoke that appears briefly and then disappears" (James 4:14). Consider, first of all, the impact that such a verse has when we read it in our society, in which the average life expectancy is seventy-eight. It hardly ruffles a feather. Then imagine reading this same verse in an African society in which the average life expectancy has now fallen below forty. When you think of a Global-South congregation, whether it be Protestant or Catholic, think of this age profile: A congregation with an average age of twenty and where the pastor is an "elderly" man of twenty-seven or twenty-eight years of age—the phrase "Repent, the end is nigh" is a literal statement of fact. You can then understand the impact that such a sermon has on the growth of Christianity in these societies.

I once heard a talk by Archbishop Bernard Malango, who is head of the Anglican Church in Central Africa. It made a deep impression on me because, for the first time in my life, I heard an archbishop threaten to go on strike. What was his complaint? "Every week," he said, "I get a request: 'Archbishop, come and consecrate a new church for us.' You know what's going to happen but you go anyway. As you drive along, there are hundreds of people cheering—all new members of the church. You get to the new church and consecrate it. Then they do it to you. They turn to you and say: 'Oh Archbishop, while you're here, could you possibly consecrate another new church?' Sometimes you end up doing *three*. It's more than any archbishop who is human can stand."

He went on to share two other things. First, he informed me that no member of the clergy had been paid in over six months. Second, he has never presided at a funeral where there were less than twelve bodies. When you consider the overwhelming nature of such poverty and the universal presence of such death, you have a better idea of what this means for the growth of Christianity. You can better understand the attraction of John 10:10, a verse that has been described as the life-verse of the African continent: "I come so that they might have life and have it more abundantly." In such a context, life does not refer merely to spiritual life; it means material life and material well-being. Otherwise, faith is empty. Healing and the welfare of body and mind go together. Otherwise, religion is false.

As many of the communities in the Global South testify, this notion of "healing" holds an important place in these communities. Indeed, healing is a predominant word in their understanding of Christianity; an example describes this well: During a healing service in Uganda, a country that will probably be one of the great Christian nations in terms of population by the middle of the century, a woman reported that she had been healed of a spinal ailment. Upon hearing this, people in the congregation spontaneously started to stand up and recount their own stories of an experience of healing. We listened to countless stories of how people had been healed of various ailments. Finally, in an effort to end the service, a deacon listed various ailments, asking each time for a show of hands of how many people had experienced a healing of that particular disease. Dozens of people raised their hands, testifying to healings from sundry ailments. Astonishingly, this healing service occurred in a Catholic church. Furthermore, these miracles occurred during the Exposition of the Blessed Sacrament.

Our Western labels do not apply to Christians in the Global South. If you ask a Nigerian member of the Anglican Church—an outrageously successful Church that counted 5 million members back in 1978, 18 million members today, and a projected 36 million members by 2025[9]—whether they are evangelical, Catholic, or Charismatic, they will answer each question with an absolute and sincere "yes." Their disregard for denominational labels is partly the result of the presence of other religions in these areas. Consequently, differences between Christians become less significant. What we call the Charismatic or Pentecostal style prevails in Churches across the board in these countries, including Catholic and Anglican Churches.

This openness to the charismatic gifts such as healing prevails even in one of my favorite churches, a particular Mennonite church in Ethiopia. For many years, I tried to graph the membership of this church, but the task became impossible because its membership growth kept going off the charts. Recently the African administrator for this church was meeting with some Canadian visitors. "We're shocked," he said. "Our church last year grew by 13 percent." Of course, the Canadians were duly impressed. "Yes, we certainly understand that you would be shocked," they replied. "Yes," the African administrator continued, "but what am I going to tell the board? They were expecting a 15 percent growth." Normally, healing does not occupy a prominent place in the Mennonite Church. Yet, Jesus preached a revolutionary message in Luke 4 when he announced that he had come to proclaim liberty to captives, to give sight to the blind, and to set captives free. His sermon in the synagogue of Nazareth contains two core ideas of Christianity: liberation and deliverance. In this country, liberation is an idea that is often associated with advocates of the theology of liberation, who are on the Left, and deliverance is an idea associated with Pentecostals, who are on the Right. However, such associations are meaningless to a Christian from Africa or Latin America. They know that deliverance and liberation is the same thing.

Not long ago, a white, middle-class, Adventist pastor from the United States was visiting an Adventist congregation in South Africa. The South African congregation was located in an area where people were not used to seeing white faces. In fact, it was regarded as an area that was dangerous for white people to enter. The church was surprised by his visit, but welcomed him with open arms. When word of his presence reached the pastor in charge of the congregation, the pastor made an announcement that, he assumed, would be received as an honor: "My friends, I have wonderful news for you. Pastor Smith has come to visit us all the way from the United States. I will ask him to conduct tonight's exorcism." Picture the consternation that this announcement caused for the visiting pastor! How many seminaries here in the United States—or in the entire Western world for that matter—prepare its graduates to deal with issues concerning healing and spiritual warfare? However, in the Global South, if you do not have a healing ministry that occupies a prominent place in your congregation, people will leave your church and go to others where they *will* find a healing ministry. I am not suggesting that we give up modern medicine. To the contrary, I am saying that we need to place modern medicine in a spiritual context. We need to understand the religious and sacramental underpinnings that drive the creativity and inquisitiveness that have given us the range of modern developments we enjoy, such as antisepsis, antibiotics, cataract surgery, and chemotherapy. There is often a religious impulse behind these developments. But let us also be prepared to present people in the Church a message of healing when they are looking for it.

Jim Wallis, a well-known Protestant author, once argued that if you take references to the poor out of the Bible, not much is left.[10] He is absolutely right. At the same time, though, if you also take references to healing, exorcism, angels, and demons out of the New Testament, you are left with an extremely thin pamphlet. People tend to read the Bible in different ways—but always in a way that makes sense to them. Francisco Goldman, a contemporary author, once observed that if you live in Africa or Central America, so much of what happens in the New Testament, particularly in the gospels, could describe your own world. "Guatemala certainly feels biblical. Sheep, swine, donkeys, serpents—

these are everywhere, as are centurions, all manner of wandering false prophets, pharisees, lepers, and whores. The poor, rural, mainly Mayan landscape has an aura of the miraculous....[It] is the perfect backdrop for religious parables about fields, both barren and fertile, fruits and harvests, hunger and plenty."[11] In such an environment, you suddenly begin to read the Bible with fresh eyes because you are trying to evangelize people who come from a society that regards the Bible as the story of their own lives.

Musimbi Kanyoro, a Kenyan scholar who is a prominent feminist author, has made an observation along these same lines: "Those cultures which are far removed from biblical culture run the risk of reading the Bible as fiction."[12] Reading the Bible as fiction might seem strange to us, but it is certainly a temptation in our modern culture. But when you read the Bible with the eyes of the Global South, when you read the Bible with *hungry* eyes, you see it in a different light. You begin to see, for example, that much of the Bible concerns food, so it becomes impossible to discuss the sacramental meaning of food again without understanding what food really means. Consider what food means in our society—a society where the main food-related story during the last couple of years has been an alleged obesity epidemic. Then read a biblical prayer that is popular in the Churches of Africa and Asia, the *Magnificat* with its awesome vision of a society in which the mighty are put down from their thrones, a society in which God feeds everybody while turning away the rich empty-handed. Suddenly you see food with new eyes!

I have heard many different versions of the blessing before meals, but I would like to share a common blessing before meals from a house church in rural China: "Today food is not easy to come by. God gives it to us. After we eat it, we will not be sick. God protects us so that we can have the next meal. He protects it so everything is prosperous and we have peace. All of our family members from young to old need the protection from God." The spirit of the New Testament Church is alive in this prayer. Imagine a group of Christians whose faith was born in a society where there is hunger and uncertainty, where today's food is not easy to come by, and for which there is no reliable source of food. It helps us understand the message behind many texts in the Bible; it helps us understand the power of a parable in presenting such a message; and perhaps it helps us understand the appeal of the Bible's

Wisdom literature with which we might have lost touch. Let's face it: Proverbs no longer hold a high reputation in our society. In fact, Forrest Gump might be the most famous fictional spinner of proverbs in our contemporary culture. Wisdom literature has enormous appeal to the Churches of the Global South because it is designed for a society based on transience and uncertainty.

Recently a British publishing house created a new series called *Revelations* consisting of the books of the Bible printed as a series of small books with introductions written by prestigious religious thinkers. The most popular book in the series was the Epistle of James, for which the great religious leader, the Dalai Lama, wrote the introduction. He essentially said: "Look, I know very little about Christianity. I know a great deal about Buddhism. This is a wonderful Buddhist text because it speaks to our society." This book, by the way, has proved to be a very successful evangelistic tool in Asia.

When I wrote my book *The Next Christendom*, I received some very strange responses to it. Many were favorable, but one of the most negative responses I received was from a woman who belonged to the Episcopal Church—a very well-heeled, aristocratic-looking woman. She made an interesting yet naïve comment: "You describe how we see in the Global South this new kind of Christianity. It's a very passionate, very enthusiastic Christianity. It's almost like a return to the Christianity of the first centuries—a primitive Christianity. Tell me: as Americans, as Christians, and as Episcopalians, what can we do to stop this?" Unfortunately, this attitude pervades much of the Western Church today. There is a fear of a Christianity that takes the Bible seriously, especially in a way that we might describe as fundamentalist—a label that we, in our American culture, often associate with a particular political package. But we need to resist such labels. We need to take seriously the approaches that we encounter among our brothers and sisters from Asia, Africa, and Latin America, especially in terms of healing, spiritual warfare, and a literal definition of evil. We Euro-American Christians have to take stock of what we believe and see where it comes from. What is Christian and what is cultural and intrinsic to our Western culture? If, for example, you ask some of the pastors of these African churches where they derive their "strange and bizarre" ideas, they will simply smile at you and patiently explain that they are found in the Book of Acts, where they are quite commonplace. It is good to recall that Christianity reached Europe through St. Paul, who had a vision in a dream and whose concept of the Church was akin to that of these African pastors.

I would suggest that the Bible, when read through "Third-World" eyes, represents a superb evangelistic tool. But, we have to go a long, long way intellectually to reach common ground. The good news, however, is that we do not have to go a long way physically in order to do so. The world has come here. The Global South is here. We once spoke about a mission *ad gentes.* Now we are in the second phase: the *gentes* are here. Personally, I believe we are living through what is potentially a greater age of change and growth in Christianity than the era of the Reformation and Catholic Reformation. This is an important time. What we as Euro-Americans have to decide is where we want to be in the picture of a world where 80 percent of Catholics are not Euro-American. Welcome to the fringe!

NOTES

1. Status of Global Mission, 2005, at http://www.globalchristianity.org/resources.htm. For future projections, see David B. Barrett, George T. Kurian, and Todd M. Johnson, *World Christian Encyclopedia,* 2nd ed. (New York: Oxford University Press, 2001), 12–15.

2. Barrett et al., *World Christian Encyclopedia.* My demographic projections are drawn from two sources, respectively the U.S. Census Bureau and the United Nations. U.S. government figures can be found through the U.S. Department of Commerce, Bureau of the Census, International Database, online at http://www.census.gov/ipc/www/id brank.html. United Nation figures are online at http://www.popin.org/.

3. John L. Allen, "Global South Will Shape the Future Catholic Church," *National Catholic Reporter,* October 7, 2005.

4. All figures are drawn from *The Official Catholic Directory 1999;* John L. Allen, "Faith, Hope and Heroes," *National Catholic Reporter,* February 23, 2001.

5. Allen, "Global South Will Shape the Future Catholic Church."

6. Rogelio Saenz, "The Changing Demographics of Roman Catholics" (2005), at http://www.prb.org/Template.cfm?Section=PRB

&template=/ContentManagement/ContentDisplay.cfm&ContentID=
12740.

7. Barrett et al., *World Christian Encyclopedia.*

8. Barrett et al., *World Christian Encyclopedia.*

9. Barrett et al., *World Christian Encyclopedia.*

10. Jim Wallis, *God's Politics* (San Francisco: HarperSanFrancisco, 2005).

11. Francisco Goldman, "The Gospel According to Matthew," in Canongate Books, comp., *Revelations: Personal Responses to the Books of the Bible* (London: Canongate Books, 2005), 210.

12. Musimbi Kanyoro, "Reading the Bible from an African Perspective," *ER* 51, no. 1 (1999): 18–24.

Contributors

Steven Boguslawski, OP, holds a doctorate from Yale in both scripture and systematic theology. He has served as academic dean at the Dominican House of Studies in Washington, DC, president-rector of Sacred Heart Major Seminary in the archdiocese of Detroit, and acting director of the Pope John Paul II Cultural Center in Washington, DC. Fr. Boguslawski is regent of studies for the Dominican Province of St. Joseph and is the author of *Thomas Aquinas and the Jews* (Paulist Press).

Avery Cardinal Dulles, SJ, is the Laurence J. McGinley Professor of Religion and Society at Fordham University in New York City. He holds a doctorate in sacred theology from the Pontifical Gregorian University in Rome. He entered the Jesuit Order in 1946, was ordained in 1956, and in 2001 became a cardinal of the Catholic Church.

Cardinal Dulles has served on the faculty of Woodstock College and the Catholic University of America. He has authored over seven hundred articles on theological topics and has published twenty-one books. Cardinal Dulles is past president of the Catholic Theological Society, has served on the International Theological Commission, and is currently an advisor to the Committee on Doctrine of the National Conference of Catholic Bishops.

Francis Cardinal George, OMI, entered the Missionary Oblates of Mary Immaculate in 1957 and was ordained a priest in 1963. After serving as vicar general of the Oblates of Mary for twelve years, he was appointed bishop of Yakima in 1990, archbishop of Portland in 1996, and the eighth archbishop of Chicago in 1997. Pope John Paul II named him a cardinal of the Catholic Church in 1998.

Cardinal George has served on numerous ecclesial congregations and advisory councils. He is currently a member of the Congregation for Divine Worship and the Discipline of the Sacraments, and the Congregation for the Evangelization of Peoples. Cardinal George holds an STD in ecclesiology from the Pontifical University Urbaniana in Rome, and a PhD in American philosophy from Tulane University,

New Orleans. Cardinal George has taught at five universities and has published scores of theological articles and reviews.

Edwin I. Hernández holds a PhD in sociology from the University of Notre Dame. In 1986, he earned an MDiv degree from the Seventh-day Adventist Theological Seminary at Andrews University. Throughout his career as a researcher, university educator, and administrator, Dr. Hernández has made major contributions to research on the role of religion in U.S. Latino communities. In 2002, he launched the Center for the Study of Latino Religion within the Institute for Latino Studies at the University of Notre Dame. The center's mission is to serve as a national center and clearinghouse for ecumenical, social-scientific study of the U.S. Latino church, its leadership, and the interaction between religion and community.

Dr. Hernández has published research of interest to both academic and pastoral audiences, including four coauthored books and numerous articles and reports. His work bridges diverse cultures, denominations, and disciplines.

Rebecca Burwell, who assisted Dr. Hernández with his research, is an assistant professional specialist and project manager of the Chicago Latino Congregations Study at the Center for the Study of Latino Religion of the Institute for Latino Studies of the University of Notre Dame.

Jeffrey Smith, who assisted Dr. Hernández with his research, is a graduate student in the department of sociology and a research assistant for the Center for the Study of Latino Religion at the Institute for Latino Studies at the University of Notre Dame.

Philip Jenkins received his doctorate in history from the University of Cambridge in 1978. Since 1980, he has taught at Penn State University and currently holds the rank of Distinguished Professor of History and Religious Studies. He is the author of twenty books, including *The New Anti-Catholicism: The Last Acceptable Prejudice* (2003); *Decade of Nightmares: The End of the 1960s and the Making of Eighties America* (2006); and *The New Faces of Christianity: Believing the Bible in the Global South* (2006).

Francis Martin is a priest of the archdiocese of Washington. He has taught in the United States at Catholic University, the Dominican House of Studies, the Franciscan University of Steubenville, and the

John Paul II Institute, and abroad at the Gregorian University and Ecole Biblique et Archéologique Française. In 2002, Fr. Martin accepted the Chair of Catholic-Jewish Theological Studies at the Intercultural Forum of the Pope John Paul II Cultural Center, and then became research fellow there in Catholic biblical studies. In 2004, he was named the Adam Cardinal Maida Chair in Sacred Scripture at Sacred Heart Major Seminary. Fr. Martin has written eight books and approximately three hundred articles. His recent works are *The Life Changer; The Feminist Question: Feminist Theology in the Light of Christian Tradition;* and *The Fire in the Cloud.*

Ralph Martin has been a leader in renewal movements in the Catholic Church for many years. He is the president of Renewal Ministries, a Catholic organization devoted to renewal and evangelization throughout the world. He is also assistant professor of theology at Sacred Heart Major Seminary and director of graduate theology programs in the new evangelization there. His latest book is *The Fulfillment of All Desire: A Guidebook for the Journey to God Based on the Wisdom of the Saints.*

Marc Montminy is pastor of St. Marie Parish in Manchester, New Hampshire. He has a broad experience in parish renewal. The story of his parish is told in a collection of essays, *John Paul II and the New Evangelization: How You Can Share the Good News with Others.*

Richard John Neuhaus is president of the Institute on Religion and Public Life and editor-in-chief of the Institute's publication, *First Things: A Monthly Journal of Religion, Culture, and Public Life.* Among his best known books are *Freedom for Ministry; The Naked Public Square: Religion and Democracy in America; The Catholic Moment: The Paradox of the Church in the Postmodern World;* and, with Rabbi Leon Klenicki, *Believing Today: Jew and Christian in Conversation.* In 1995 he edited, with Charles Colson, *Evangelicals & Catholics Together: Toward A Common Mission.* His most recent book is *Catholic Matters: Confusion, Controversy, and the Splendor of Truth* (2006).

As a Lutheran clergyman, he was senior pastor of a low-income black parish in Brooklyn, New York, for seventeen years . He received his formal education in Ontario and in the United States and is a graduate of Concordia Theological Seminary, St. Louis, Missouri. In 1991 he was ordained a priest in the archdiocese of New York by Cardinal John O'Connor.

Robert S. Rivers, CSP, is vice president and director of parish missions for the Paulist National Catholic Evangelization Association (PNCEA) in Washington, DC. He is deeply committed to developing the ministry of evangelization. For the past eleven years, he has functioned as a presenter on various aspects of evangelization at national, regional, and diocesan conferences. His expertise in parish life comes from more than twenty-five years of pastoral experience, the last fifteen years serving as pastor of Paulist parishes in Greensboro, North Carolina, and in Los Angeles, California.

In addition to conducting parish evangelization missions, Fr. Rivers supervises twenty-five PNCEA missionary teams that conduct parish missions throughout the country. He served for eight years as a campus minister at state universities in Minnesota and Texas, and is the author of *From Maintenance to Mission, Evangelization and the Revitalization of the Church* (Paulist Press).